Going to the Sourc

Coils to the Source

Going to the Sources

A Guide to Historical Research and Writing

FIFTH EDITION

Anthony Brundage

WILEY-BLACKWELL

A John Wiley & Sons, Ltd., Publication

This fifth edition first published 2013
© John Wiley & Sons, Ltd.
Edition history: Harlan Davidson, Inc. (1e, 1989; 2e, 1997; 3e, 2002; 4e, 2008)

Harlan Davidson, Inc. was acquired by John Wiley & Sons in May 2012.

Registered Office
John Wiley & Sons Ltd., The Atrium, Southern Gate, Chichester, West Sussex,
PO19 8SQ, UK

Editorial Offices
350 Main Street, Malden, MA 02148-5020, USA
9600 Garsington Road, Oxford, OX4 2DQ, UK
The Atrium, Southern Gate, Chichester, West Sussex, PO19 8SQ, UK

For details of our global editorial offices, for customer services, and for
information about how to apply for permission to reuse the copyright material
in this book please see our website at www.wiley.com/wiley-blackwell.

The right of Anthony Brundage to be identified as the author of this work has
been asserted in accordance with the UK Copyright, Designs, and Patents Act
1988.

Library of Congress Cataloging-in-Publication Data
Brundage, Anthony, 1938–
  Going to the sources : a guide to historical research and writing /
Anthony Brundage. – Fifth edition.
     pages cm
  Includes bibliographical references and index.
  ISBN 978-1-118-51531-0 (paperback : alkaline paper)   1. History–
Methodology.   2. History–Research.   3. History–Research–Data
processing.   4. Historiography.   I. Title.
  D16.B893 2013
  907.2–dc23
                        2012036173

A catalog record for this book is available from the British Library.

Cover image: Utrecht University Library © Rene de Wit Rene de Wit/Arcaid/
Corbis
Cover design by Simon Levy

Set in 10/13 pt Meridian by Toppan Best-set Premedia Limited
Printed in Malaysia by Ho Printing (M) Sdn Bhd

1   2013

To My Students

Contents

Preface to the Fifth Edition

This book developed out of a course on history methods that I have taught to upper division history majors for many years. As anyone who has taught a methodology course can attest, it can be either a uniquely rewarding or a deeply frustrating experience; usually it is both. Typically students approach the course with some apprehension. Up to this point their academic encounters with history have been chiefly in the form of lecture-discussion courses, a format with which they feel relatively secure. In the History Methods class they suddenly find themselves on unfamiliar terrain, confronted with new, sometimes perplexing challenges. Fortunately, often mingled with this apprehension is a sense of excitement about the prospect of achieving new levels of understanding the discipline, as well as of acquiring a new set of research and writing skills. It was in the hope of fostering the excitement, allaying the apprehension, and developing these skills that I undertook the writing of this book.

Central to my own sense of the excitement of history is an appreciation of it as an open-ended and dynamic field. Developing that awareness in others is an important source of satisfaction for me as a teacher of history. I have therefore structured my course and this book around the concept of history as a dynamic process. The common tendency to view history as fixed and static is best overcome by exploring the ways in which historians actually go about examining the past, constantly searching for fresh patterns and meanings, and developing new methodologies to achieve them. Accordingly, an introductory chapter on historiography (the history of history writing) sets the stage for a discussion of the types of historical sources and of the organization of the historical profession in Chapter 2.

Chapter 3, on how to locate your sources, is the central chapter as far as research methods are concerned. It is a detailed, practical guide through the various resources that enable you to identify and obtain the most important books, articles, essays, and other materials relating to your topic. Once this knowledge is acquired, the essential bibliography on any historical topic can be located readily. Fostering one's ability to operate as a competent, self-directed researcher is one of the major goals of this book.

Chapter 4 explains how to give any work of history a critical reading; it provides you with the tools to grasp the structure of the work and the author's main interpretive points. By comparing two books seemingly on the same topic, it shows the different approaches and strategies historians deploy in creating their work. It also explains the major points one should include when writing a book review. Chapter 5, entirely new to this edition, considers the uses of visual media by historians, both in enhancing scholarship and in posing some critical challenges to authors as well as to readers.

Chapters 6 and 7 explore the methods of writing two common assignments: the historiographic essay (an annotated example of which is included) and the research paper. This follows the sequence of my own teaching, in which a historiographic essay (based chiefly on secondary sources) is the centerpiece of the History Methods class, while a longer research paper (using primary as well as secondary sources) is assigned in the Senior Thesis and Seminar. Chapter 7 recapitulates some of the major points made in the book, in particular the theme of the open-ended nature of history. The achievement of creative insights and analyses is shown to be closely linked to the concept of history as a dynamic intellectual discipline.

Online databases for historical researchers have improved enormously in recent years, as have college library gateways to these databases. Internet research has become such a vital and central component of the historian's toolkit that this edition gives it extended treatment. The book concludes with five helpful appendices, four of which provide easy-to-follow examples of formatting for footnotes, endnotes, and bibliography entries, while a final one lists commonly used abbreviations in scholarly works.

1

The Ever-Changing Shape and Texture of the Past

Static and Dynamic Concepts of History

A conversation I had at a cocktail party years ago made me acutely aware of some common misconceptions about my chosen field of study. After being introduced to a psychologist, I listened with keen interest to his enthusiastic account of some of the latest approaches and interpretations in his discipline. Having expostulated on this topic with obvious relish, he said, "I don't suppose there's much new going on in your field." Stunned by this remark, I scrutinized his face for signs of either humor or intentional offense. Seeing neither, I was forced to conclude that he genuinely believed history to be a passive, if not dormant, discipline. I attempted to disabuse him of this unfortunate view by explaining some of the recent – and important – developments in history: social history, women's history, cliometrics, psychohistory, microhistory, and postmodernism. The mention of psychohistory produced a detectable flash of interest, and I would like to think that he has since begun to question his assumption that history is a dull, lifeless chronicle.

Going to the Sources: A Guide to Historical Research and Writing, Fifth Edition.
Anthony Brundage.
© 2013 John Wiley & Sons, Ltd. Published 2013 by John Wiley & Sons, Ltd.

Reflecting later on this encounter, I realized that my companion's attitude was by no means unusual, even among highly educated persons. The reasons for this are readily apparent. The popular conception of history simply as a record of past events seems to have the idea of history's basic unchangeability as an obvious corollary. Many see history as a vast array of facts, largely political and military in character, arranged more or less chronologically. Thus conceived, history is unalterable, except through the occasional unearthing of a lost city or the discovery of a trunk full of letters in an attic. At its best, it is an exciting and vivid costume drama; at its worst, it becomes a tedious, turgid catalog of dates and names designed to torment the young. We should not be surprised that it is the latter viewpoint that predominates. Not only is modern American culture remorselessly present-minded, but quite often the way in which history is taught in our precollegiate schools only confirms its reputation as dull.

Things tend to improve at college level, where those who have not already developed an attitude of unremitting hostility toward history often discover that it offers them an exciting new set of intellectual challenges and vistas. Yet, even at this level, introductory courses sometimes only solidify students' negative attitudes. This is not a matter of bad teaching; knowledgeable, enthusiastic, and articulate history teachers abound at every level. The problem lies in presenting history as a story with a fixed plot and cast of characters. It is true that this approach is natural and to some extent unavoidable, particularly with students who receive their first systematic exposure to history. But it is also possible, indeed critically important, to offer at least a glimpse of a very different concept: history as a dynamic process. By this I mean a rich, varied, evolving intellectual system that allows us to achieve a deeper and better understanding of our world, indeed of ourselves. In this vein history still deals with the past, but it conceptualizes a past in constant dialog with an ever-advancing present, one that responds to new questions and reveals fresh insights into the human condition. This is history as it is understood (and enjoyed) by professional historians, and it is high time that others were let in on the secret.

Obviously this concept of history stands in sharp contrast to the static one that prevails when we think of history merely as a fixed story. In the former, the past becomes kaleidoscopic, offering different answers to each inquirer. This should not be taken to mean that every person can fashion whatever he or she wishes and call it history. There are rigorous procedures one must observe in the framing of historical questions, in the selection and interpretation of sources, and in the presentation of one's findings. Moreover, the pursuit of objectivity, though impossible to achieve fully, must remain a central concern of the historian. Not everyone finds the dynamic concept of history appealing; there is, after all, something comforting in the notion that the past is unchangeable. A shift from the static to the dynamic can be as disconcerting as our recent awakening (and I mean "recent" in terms of natural history) to the fact that the *terra firma* on which we walk is in fact an array of seething, grinding tectonic plates (an example all too familiar to a native Californian). The difference, of course, is that, while shifting tectonic plates seem to promise only devastation in the form of violent earthquakes and tsunamis, the concept of a dynamic historical past holds the promise of intellectual growth.

Revising Our View of the Past

Rather than simply presenting a rigidly fixed view of the past, historians constantly search for fresh sources, approaches, methodological tools, and interpretations, in an effort to offer an ever-new past to whatever the present is. It may be more precise to say that historians offer us a multitude of new pasts, since each historian's view of the past is at least slightly different from another's, and sometimes dramatically so. In other words a vigorous, many-sided debate among scholars is not only unavoidable but essential to the discipline. Even when differences are subtle, they can be important. When an interpretation entails a more sweeping challenge to an established way of interpreting a past event, process, or person, we call it revisionist.

Revisionism, together with less extensive shifts in approaches and interpretations, has been practiced since at least the time of the ancient Greeks, as anyone who has examined the history of historiography (that is, of history writing) will know. Revisionism has, however, become particularly pronounced in the last few centuries, with the dramatic transformations that have taken place in social, economic, and political life. As the pace of change quickens and the magnitude of change increases, a corresponding pressure arises that we revise our presently held accounts of the past. This happens because one of the most fundamental dimensions of our identity is provided by history and, as we change, so must it, too. When a young United States was mainly an agrarian society with few large cities, no complex technology, and no vital role to play in the world, one kind of history sufficed. As the nation grew, became industrialized, and developed an array of perplexing social problems, Americans needed to ask new questions about their past: What was life like on the frontier, and how had these experiences shaped the development of our national character? What was the historical experience of hitherto disempowered or exploited groups: African Americans, American Indians, Hispanics, Asians, and women? How did mass immigration affect politics, society, culture, and the economy? How did the different social classes interact historically, and how and why are the old patterns changing? How was the United States' posture vis-à-vis the rest of the world changing? These are only a few of the questions that have been posed by generations of historians since the late nineteenth century. Not surprisingly, a multiplicity of new approaches and interpretations has been offered in response, and hitherto neglected records and remnants of the past have become primary-source material.

Americans did not, of course, initiate these new ways of looking at the past. Many European societies had begun to experience social and economic change much earlier, and this was reflected in their historical accounts. The *philosophes* of the European Enlightenment developed a decidedly revisionist view of history and used it to great effect in their campaign against ignorance, superstition, and tyranny. Writers like Voltaire and Gibbon broke with long-established tendencies to write reverentially about states, rulers, and legal and ecclesiastical institutions. Their works, still rightly regarded as great classics in the writing of history, served as manifestos in the eighteenth-century struggle to advance the cause of liberty and reason.

New Forms of Historical Consciousness

With the advent of the Industrial Revolution and the attendant political unrest and demographic change at the end of the eighteenth century, some writers were moved to ask novel questions about the past. Thomas Malthus, that "gloomy" economist who began to point with alarm to the rapid and accelerating growth of population, complained that "the histories of mankind which we possess are, in general, histories only of the higher classes." He went on to suggest the composition of a history of the habits and mores of the general population on the basis of accurate statistical information. Malthus was well aware of the massive intellectual labors that would have to be expended on such a project, but he nonetheless called upon future scholars to shoulder the burden:

> A satisfactory history of this kind, of one people and of one period, would require the constant and minute attention of many observing minds in local and general remarks on the state of the lower classes of society, and the causes that influenced it; and to draw accurate inferences upon this subject, a succession of such historians for some centuries would be necessary.[1]

Thus, almost two hundred years ago, Malthus outlined an agenda for the diligent historical demographers and social historians of our time, whose labors are bearing rich fruit. Fortunately the invention of the computer has significantly shortened the time he predicted would be required for such investigations.

The miseries thrust upon humanity by the early Industrial Revolution, coupled with the rise of a large and militant working

---

[1] Thomas Malthus, *An Essay on Population* (London: J. M. Dent, 1952 [first published 1798]), vol. 1, 16.

class, prompted others to look for the historic roots of social conflict. Karl Marx is, beyond question, the most important of these commentators, and many historical studies have been immensely enriched by his powerful and trenchant analyses. When he and Friedrich Engels issued *The Communist Manifesto* in 1848, that text was intended as a clarion call to arms, not as a work of scholarship. But the manifesto's assertions that the economic organization of society is the key to the past and that human history is driven by class struggle represent perhaps the most sweeping revisionist claims ever offered.

Marx's insistence that each historical epoch can be properly understood only by reference to its economic and material bases has profoundly altered the discipline of history. Virtually all subsequent historians, most of whom would object to being described as Marxists, are deeply in Marx's debt. This is not a question of embracing Marxism as an ideology or of accepting its critique of capitalism and its vision of the future – elements that can be readily detached from the Marxist perspective on the past. The point is that Marx, like Malthus, forced people to question whether humanity is really well served by confining its historical attention to the doings of kings, statesmen, and generals – a questioning that, admittedly, had been initiated earlier, by writers like Voltaire. It is by no means the case that political history, military history, or biography has withered on the vine as a result of these new perspectives. Indeed some of the best work being done in those more traditional forms of history is the better for taking economic and social forces into account. Overall, the juxtaposition of the old forms with the new perspectives has created a complex, multifaceted debate – another manifestation of the vitality of history as a process.

Toward a "People's History"

I do not mean to suggest that without Malthus or Marx historians would have continued in their accustomed mold. Society was being transformed in too many ways for this to have been possible; the emergence of a variety of new approaches to historical inquiry was inevitable. One example is provided by a maverick English clergyman named John Richard Green, who wrote a very influential book published in 1874 and entitled *A Short History of the English People.* In the preface to his work, Green declared:

> I have preferred to pass lightly and briefly over the details of foreign wars and diplomacies, the personal adventures of kings and nobles, the pomp of courts, or the intrigues of favourites, and to dwell at length on the incidents of that constitutional, intellectual, and social advance in which we read the history of the nation itself.[2]

The striking inclusion in the title of Green's book was the word "people": the author clearly believed that he was shifting the spotlight away from historic elites to the mass of the population.

While many consider Green's *Short History of the English People* less innovative than he claimed, the book was enormously successful, because the late nineteenth-century public thought it was breaking new ground in a way they considered necessary and important. It was reprinted 16 times before the second edition appeared, posthumously, in 1887. Numerous pirated editions were published in the United States, and before the end of the century Italian, French, German, Russian, and Chinese translations had appeared. Such an astonishing publishing success was due to something more than Green's literary gifts. Much of the world was then in the grip of vigorous populist and nationalist impulses, and the idea of a history of a "people" proved irresistibly attractive. It was a history, or rather a kind of history, whose time had come.

Needless to say, Green's *Short History* did not put an end to revisionism – no work ever has, or will. It might even be said to have intensified the ferment and accelerated the revisionist process. Making the "people" the centerpiece of historical inquiry

[2]   John Richard Green, *A Short History of the English People* (New York: Harper & Brothers, 1899 [first published 1874]), xvii.

begged a number of essential questions. Just who was, or were, the "people"? Was it the entire population or some segment of it – workers, or the middle class perhaps? Was the focus to be on city dwellers or on peasants? Should ethnic or religious minorities be taken into account? What about women – never a minority but hitherto ignored by historians – was their story to be considered, too? Furthermore, Green's focus on the English people implied that national entities were appropriate units of historical investigation; yet there were many others, ranging from institutions to small communities – and the latter could be confined to regions or expanded to the entire world.

Minorities and Women Enter History

Revisionist efforts to recover and develop the history of minorities have, by necessity, been undertaken in political movements for the expansion of civil rights and the attainment of economic and social equality. In the early decades of the twentieth century, the great African American historian W. E. B. DuBois stood as a major figure in the struggle for racial equality. His own writings, along with his participation in the founding of the *Journal of Negro History*, enhanced the visibility of African Americans and helped rescue their history from the patronizing or frankly racist attitudes of most white historians of the period. An expansion of interest in black history during the last several decades is obviously linked to the intensification of the struggle for civic, social, and economic equality. In revealing the historic patterns of race relations, this new body of scholarship has served to enhance the pride and clarify the goals of African Americans. Moreover, it has educated other Americans about the nature and consequences of racism, thereby fostering progress toward a society of greater justice and opportunity. Much the same can be said of the burgeoning scholarship on the history of Hispanics, American Indians, and other ethnic minorities.

Women's history has been particularly active during the last few decades, and, as with the history of ethnic minorities, its creation is correlated to vigorous political and social movements. Since historical invisibility is a virtually universal corollary to powerlessness, the campaign to establish gender equality necessarily required a historical component. Just as the "people" in the title of Green's *Short History* served as a rallying cry for populist and national groups many years ago, June Sochen's title *Herstory* (1974) did the same for the women's movement. Although many important works in women's history had appeared before, *Herstory*, the title of this volume, evoked in a single word the need for a story very different from those that had been told for so long by male historians.[3]

It should not be assumed, however, that histories of minorities or of women are designed or undertaken merely to serve as appendages to political causes. The writing of these histories requires satisfying the same demanding criteria regarding the evaluation of sources, the marshaling of evidence, and the deployment of literary skill upon which all histories rely. This takes a blend of diligence, skepticism, imagination, judiciousness, and humor that pays big dividends to historians in any field. Nor should these newer bodies of scholarship be seen as representing some sort of ethnic or gender-related orthodoxy. None is any more monolithic than any other field of history. Indeed, some of the most vigorous and interesting debates within the profession occur in these newer, albeit politically charged, areas.

One important point of disagreement within minority history involves the same type of concern as the one manifested in the nineteenth century over whether to focus on an elite group or on the entire population. Many of the earlier studies tended to concentrate on the achievements of extraordinary persons. Critics have charged that, whatever the merits of these works in producing positive role models, they often serve to obscure the historical realities around the lives of the masses of the disempowered. As a result, there has been a shift in women's and minority history toward incorporating some of the methods and approaches of

[3] June Sochen, *Herstory: A Woman's View of American History* (New York: Alfred Publishing, 1974).

social history. This particular application of "history from below" exemplifies not only revisionism but also the process of cross-fertilization among various fields of history. Furthermore, while women's history continues to exist as an important field, there has been a broadening from its base into "gender studies" – a field devoted to investigating the ways in which gender identities, both overt and latent, have shaped all aspects of the human experience.

So far, the examples of historical scholarship we have examined, while exhibiting the concept of history as process, can be fitted into the "history as story" format. That is, in most cases the historian renders a narrative structure in which a sequence of connected events occurring within a particular span of time is analyzed so as to create pattern and meaning. Even when large social aggregates like classes or ethnic groups rather than individuals are the centerpiece of the story, usually they can still be made to function as (individualized) characters in a complex story. Marx's scheme of history, with its rising bourgeoisie deployed (at one stage) against a crumbling feudal nobility, is a good example. The unfolding of the Marxist story of class conflict is marked by such significant events or movements as the rapid growth of towns, the Protestant Reformation, the invention of the steam engine, the French Revolution, and the "scramble for Africa" by colony-hungry European powers in the late nineteenth century. But the twentieth century witnessed the emergence of varieties of history that largely abandon the investigation of change over time. We will briefly examine two of them: the Annales School and cliometrics.

The Annales School and Cliometrics

A historical journal established in France in 1929 provided the forum for a new kind of historical scholarship: one that aimed at nothing less than recapturing the totality of human experience. By employing the methods and techniques of social sciences, the scholars connected with this new enterprise sought to delineate all aspects of past societies, placing an emphasis on those enduring patterns of culture that changed slowly, if at all. The mouthpiece of this new school of historians was a journal called *Annales d'histoire économique et sociale*; hence practitioners of this kind of history came to be called *annalistes*. Central to the *annalistes'* approach was a disparagement of event-oriented history. Those innumerable events that historians had charged with significance and arranged in various configurations to produce narrative accounts were regarded by the *annalistes* as mere surface ripples on the ocean of society. In the new school, the traditional concern with events was replaced by a search for society's *mentalités*, the ways of life and the values that persisted despite major political and social upheavals.

One of the foremost *annalistes* was Fernand Braudel, whose magisterial study *The Mediterranean and the Mediterranean World in the Age of Philip II* appeared in 1949. Braudel's revisionism involved not only an emphasis on persistent patterns of life but also the use of the Mediterranean basin as the setting for his analysis – as opposed to the use of some political entity like Spain or France. A favorite phrase of Braudel and other *annalistes* was *la longue durée*, a vast sweep of time during which little change occurred. Regarding the difficulty of gaining acceptance for this new and radically different perspective in the historical profession, Braudel commented:

> For the historian, accepting the *longue durée* entails a readiness to change his style, his attitudes, a whole reversal in his thinking, a whole new way of conceiving social affairs. It means becoming used to a slower tempo, which sometimes almost borders on the motionless.[4]

Although Braudel himself by no means neglected "events" altogether, it is clear that the *annaliste* approach in its purest form tends virtually to preclude any sense of history as story.

---

[4]   Fernand Braudel, *On History*, trans. Sarah Matthews (Chicago, IL: University of Chicago Press, 1980), 33.

A close partnership between historians and other social scientists is an important tenet of the Annales School. The attempt to delineate cultural patterns with little attention to change over time is an approach similar to that employed by many anthropologists and sociologists. An even newer field of history, called cliometrics – after Clio (pronounced *CLY-oh*), the Greek muse of history – evinces a similar determination to utilize social science methodologies. Cliometricians are scholars who employ quantification to reveal historical patterns and change over time. Obviously something a good deal more is requisite than an ability or willingness to count, which historians have been doing since Herodotus (the ancient Greek historian). Cliometricians use computers, sophisticated programs, and social science models in their analyses. They also tend to disparage source material that cannot be quantified, so they devalue many of the records that other historians rely on; in cliometrics these are considered "soft" or "impressionistic" evidence, to be used only reluctantly and in strict subordination to the numeric data. Clearly, only those areas of historical study for which there is an ample supply of records yielding quantifiable data are amenable to such an approach. For this reason economic history has been a particularly active area of cliometric investigation – and a particularly controversial one.

Among the most controversial of the cliometric studies is Robert Fogel and Stanley Engerman's ringingly revisionist book *Time on the Cross* (1974), a study of slavery in the United States. Deploying a formidable array of charts, graphs, and statistics, the authors set out to disprove a number of time-honored beliefs about slavery, such as its alleged inefficiency by comparison to a free economy. The picture of American slavery in *Time on the Cross* is that of a thriving, expanding institution in both its agricultural and its industrial components. Besides promoting their own revisionist view of slavery, Fogel and Engerman made sweeping claims about the ability of cliometrics to transform economic history across a broad front:

> The cliometricians have downgraded the role of technological change in American economic advance; they have controverted

the claim that railroads were necessary to the settlement and exploitation of the West; they have contended that the boom and bust of the 1830s and early 1840s were the consequences of developments in Mexico and Britain rather than the policies of Andrew Jackson; and they have rejected the contention that the Civil War greatly accelerated the industrialization of the nation.[5]

Despite this assertion, none of these new interpretations has gone unchallenged. Indeed Fogel and Engerman's work helped trigger a major counterattack, not only against some of the cliometricians' interpretations, but against much of their methodology as well. Perhaps the most vigorous assault came from Jacques Barzun, whose *Clio and the Doctors* appeared in the same year as Fogel and Engerman's study. Barzun made an eloquent plea for keeping history within the humanist tradition and for resisting the temptation to use the latest piece of technology or scientific model. And, as the title of his book indicates, Barzun was writing not only about the cliometricians but about another new group as well: the psychohistorians.[6]

Psychology and History

Psychohistory represents an attempt to apply to historical study the methods and insights developed by Sigmund Freud and other psychological theorists during the past hundred years or so. In dealing with the question of motives, historians often have to look beneath the surface, in an effort to discern the real – as opposed to the alleged – reason for an action or policy. Generally they recognize that to move beyond the manifest content of the sources tends to render such judgments tentative and problematic. Psychohistorians, however, are less disposed to be tentative

[5] Robert Fogel and Stanley L. Engerman, *Time on the Cross: The Economics of American Negro Slavery* (Boston, MA and Toronto, Canada: Little, Brown, 1974), vol. 1, 7.

[6] Jacques Barzun, *Clio and the Doctors: Psycho-History, Quanto-History, and History* (Chicago, IL: University of Chicago Press, 1974).

when it comes to making assumptions. They undertake to expose what is claimed to be the real but hitherto hidden face of the past. One of the leading practitioners of psychobiography, the late Fawn Brodie, described in her revisionist study of Thomas Jefferson the nature of the psychohistorical approach as well as the barriers to its acceptance:

> The idea that a man's inner life affects every aspect of his intellectual life and also his decision-making should need no defense today. To illuminate this relationship, however, requires certain biographical techniques that make some historians uncomfortable. One must look for feeling as well as fact, for nuance and metaphor as well as idea and action.[7]

One important distinction between psychohistory and some of the other, newer approaches to history that draw upon social science methodology is that the former is altogether compatible with history as story. Indeed it has assisted in the revival of biography, a traditional genre generally disparaged by the *annalistes* and others concerned with broad, enduring patterns of social life and culture. In some respects, psychobiography and the Annales School are opposite poles; it is hard to imagine points of focus more different than the life of an individual on the one hand and the *mentalité* of an entire civilization across a vast sweep of time on the other. Of course, psychohistorians are not necessarily biographers. The methods and insights of social psychology can uncover many other dimensions to the study of social history: the phenomenon of crowd psychology during times of political or social turbulence, for example. They can prove useful to the *annalistes*, provided that the mass psychological patterns being examined are of an enduring nature.

Microhistory and Macrohistory

In recent decades some historical scholars have produced very tightly focused studies of a single community, while others have

---

[7]   Fawn Brodie, *Thomas Jefferson: An Intimate History* (New York: Norton, 1974), 16.

written histories from a global perspective. A leading example of the former kind is the French historian Emmanuel Le Roy Ladurie's study of the medieval French village of Montaillou over a 30-year period.[8] The chance survival of Inquisition records for this village allowed the author to plumb the depths of the local peasants' views on such matters as childhood, marriage, magic, religion, and the afterlife – a kind of *annaliste* approach with an extremely local focus. As for global history, although there were important early precursors such as the great North African scholar Ibn Khaldun (1332–1406), the pioneering figure in the twentieth century was the British scholar Arnold J. Toynbee. His 12-volume *A Study of History*,[9] with its vast sweeps of time and comparisons between major civilizations, inspired others to broaden their approach far beyond the confines of the nation-state, or even of a particular culture. An especially avid disciple of Toynbee was the American historian William H. McNeill, whose numerous studies of the same type[10] have had an enormous impact on historical writing. With rapidly increasing globalization, this kind of historical scholarship is certain to expand further.

Postmodernism

The last few decades have seen the rise of a cluster of methodologies that go under the name "postmodernism." Originating in European, and especially French, literary theory, this approach represents what some have called the "linguistic turn" in historical studies. Some of the key formulators of the body of theory on which postmodernism is based are Michel Foucault, Jacques Derrida, and Jacques Lacan.

---

[8]   Emmanuel Le Roy Ladurie, *Montaillou: The Promised Land of Error*, trans. Barbara Bray (New York: George Braziller, 1978). The book was first published in French in 1975.

[9]   Arnold J. Toynbee, *A Study of History*, 12 vols. (London: Oxford University Press, 1948–61).

[10]   See, for example, William H. McNeill, *The Global Condition: Conquerors, Catastrophes, and Community* (Princeton, NJ: Princeton University Press, 1992).

A method known as "deconstructionism" lies at the heart of the postmodernist analysis of many forms of art and literature, as well as of historical literature. Essentially, a historical deconstructionist analysis explores the operation of key "texts" and "discourses" around which societies are organized. These texts and discourses, which are largely constructed to bolster the power of social elites and dominant ideologies, can range from formal political or constitutional documents through works of literature to all forms of social commentary and popular entertainment. Such "discourses," unrecognized as such by the vast majority of the society being studied, can include nonlinguistic sources as well – for instance architecture, photography, and all kinds of images. Deconstructionists endeavor to strip away the positive or idealistic façades of dominant discourses in order to expose them for what they believe them to be: tools for legitimating political, social, economic, and cultural oppression. This approach is called postmodernist in part because it challenges the essentially modern belief (dominant since the Enlightenment) that human institutions, guided by reason and science, have tended to become progressively more tolerant and humane.

In the United States postmodernism was brought forcefully to the attention of most historians in the late 1970s, through the translation into English of Michel Foucault's *Discipline and Punish*,[11] a book first published in France in 1975. This impressive, though still controversial, postmodernist analysis is concerned with the evolution of the idea of the modern prison in the eighteenth and nineteenth centuries. Whereas previous historians had tended to see marked progress in the treatment of criminals (the end of barbaric forms of execution, new standards of decency in prisons, recourse to the concept of rehabilitation), Foucault depicted the new rehabilitatory regimen instituted in prisons as being far more intrusive than the old system, and also as being destructive of the individual and totalitarian in its implications. Indeed Foucault tended to see the prison as almost a microcosm

[11]   Michel Foucault, *Discipline and Punish: The Birth of the Prison*, trans. Alan Sheridan (Harmondsworth: Penguin Books, 1979).

of modern society, whose increasingly powerful and sophisticated devices for marginalizing and suppressing deviant behavior are part of a relentless drive to produce a single acceptable human type: rational, docile, and materialistic.

There are few elements in any society that cannot be "deconstructed" to reveal the manner in which they bolster the power of elites, maintain hierarchical distinctions, and marginalize those whom the majority see as different. Postmodernism, which is prominent today in the field of cultural history, has had a particularly marked effect on women's history, gender studies, and the history of imperialism; yet it remains controversial. Critics claim that its emphasis on oppression and marginalization is a distortion of the past, and that it too readily lends itself to present-day polemical purposes and political causes, to the detriment of scholarly rigor. Another concern is that postmodernism's emphasis on the slipperiness and infinite malleability of language, together with its denial of the possibility of objectivity in our understanding of human affairs, amounts to a kind of philosophical nihilism.[12] Some of the more ideologically driven works in this genre do indeed bear out these concerns. However, a postmodernist approach, when used sensitively, selectively, and with sufficient detachment from ideological commitments and identity politics, can be a helpful tool in studying history.

A Multitude of Avenues to the Past

The foregoing examples of changes in the way historians have approached the past during the last couple of centuries were introduced in an attempt to illustrate the concept of history as a dynamic process. While the above is only a cursory survey at best, clearly "history as story" is not a dead form. In spite of the appearance of new kinds of analysis, the narrative mode of writing history is still dominant. What is crucial to grasp is that

---

[12] S. Joyce Appleby, Lynn Hunt, and Margaret Jacob, *Telling the Truth about History* (New York and London: W. W. Norton, 1995), especially 198–237.

there is an enormous variety of narrative approaches, and new ones will continue to appear. There is, quite simply, no such thing as a "definitive" treatment of any topic. Although this qualification is sometimes applied to particularly impressive works of scholarship, its application would, if taken literally, foreclose all subsequent inquiry on a given topic. Then history would indeed evolve into that static body of knowledge so often imagined by those with too little exposure to it as a discipline.

Historiography, which in its broadest sense means the history of historical writing, is a demanding and vitally important branch of the discipline of history. Students who have not taken a course in historiography before embarking upon advanced undergraduate research projects would be well advised to read some of the general works on the subject.[13] It is important to have some notion of historiography in this broad sense before turning to our discussion of bibliographic research on a given topic. Once you are engaged in research for a project, the term *historiography* will be encountered in its narrower meaning: the various ways scholars have approached and interpreted the subject(s) you have chosen to investigate. Every topic has its own historiography, and an understanding of its dimensions is essential not only for constructing a historiographic essay, but also for writing a research paper using primary sources. These are the two types of historical writing that will be explored in later chapters. Before undertaking the writing of either a historiographic essay or a research paper, however, it is necessary to know the different types of historical sources and how to find them – matters we will explore in the next two chapters.

[13]   See, for example, Ernst Breisach, *Historiography, Ancient, Medieval, and Modern*, 3rd ed. (Chicago, IL: University of Chicago Press, 2007).

2

The Nature and Variety of Historical Sources

As we saw in Chapter 1, history is an intellectual discipline marked by ongoing change and punctuated by the periodic appearance of major revisionist works. Historians are constantly reviewing and rethinking the past, discovering new patterns and meanings. In this process they depend upon the tangible remains of the past for source materials. Any remnant of the past can serve the purpose. Although written records tend to predominate as source materials in most fields of history, in some (particularly those related to ancient and medieval history) scholars rely heavily on artifacts. Such materials are of importance to those who study modern history as well. Weapons, coins, household utensils, cathedrals, statues, and films can cast as much light on the past as can diaries, letters, and newspapers. Whether these historical raw materials are written records or artifacts, we refer to them as primary sources. The written histories that historians fashion from these (primary) sources become in turn (secondary) sources for subsequent investigators.

Going to the Sources: A Guide to Historical Research and Writing, Fifth Edition.
Anthony Brundage.
© 2013 John Wiley & Sons, Ltd. Published 2013 by John Wiley & Sons, Ltd.

Primary Sources

Written primary sources can be divided into two major categories: manuscript sources and published sources. For historians, a manuscript is any handwritten or typed record or communication that has not been printed or otherwise duplicated in significant quantities for public dissemination. It can be anything, from a laundry list to the minutes of a cabinet meeting in the Oval Office. Usually manuscript materials were intended for private, or at least restricted use, although something like the notes for a speech that was never delivered would also be considered a manuscript source. A manuscript can be something as intensely personal as a diary, or something as institutional as a roster of Egyptian temple scribes. There is virtually no kind of written record that has not been used, or might someday be used, as a primary source. As social history and other new approaches to the past continue to evolve, even the seemingly most trivial or mundane remnants may acquire significance.

Manuscript sources

We will devote most of our attention to published primary sources, since undergraduate researchers in university libraries usually have only limited access to manuscript source materials. In many cases, however, there may be significant manuscript collections close at hand. Perhaps your university library has a manuscripts or a special collections department containing important materials. There may also be nearby community libraries, local historical societies, or private individuals with such resources. A look through any of these collections might prove extremely rewarding, depending on your subject. If you are researching a topic of local history, you are more likely to be afforded the opportunity to get your hands on manuscript materials. In any event, it is worthwhile to investigate the availability of manuscript collections in your locality; this may even help you choose a viable research topic, though it should be realized that access to many major manuscript collections is limited to professional historians and advanced graduate students.

Published sources

Published primary sources can be divided into two categories: (1) manuscript materials such as letters, diaries, and memoranda, usually intended as private, sometimes intimate, documents, often published after the death of their authors; and (2) materials that were intended from the outset to be printed and made public – for example newspaper articles, congressional debates, autobiographies, annual reports of corporations, and reports of the United States Census.

There are few major political figures in the modern world, particularly in the United States, whose writings have not been published. Library shelves groan with the massive collected works of our presidents and major public figures. Past leaders of other societies are also well represented, so that, when researching the activities of the wielders of power or shapers of opinion, you will usually find no shortage of published primary sources. While many of these writings were not, strictly speaking, intended for public consumption, it is scarcely surprising that they eventually appeared in published form. Those who attained high office during the last couple of centuries could hardly expect that their papers would remain confidential for very long after their death. Indeed, the measure of immortality attainable through the posthumous publication of one's collected papers is apt to be a component of political ambition. Some leaders might even have "played to posterity" at certain times; for this reason we must read and consider their papers with an additional measure of critical judgment.

The injunction to be critical of the papers of society's leaders applies with special force to personal memoirs and autobiographies written "after the fact," when these authors/subjects were at the end of their careers or in retirement. These types of published sources require interpretive care on two grounds. First, one must remember that the validity of such sources depends to a considerable extent on the author's ability to recall events that may have occurred much earlier in his or her life. Obviously one must always assume an erosion of reliability in such recollections, one that increases with the amount of time that has elapsed. As the historian Arthur M. Schlesinger Jr. (1917–2007) observed in the preface to his autobiography: "The generic title for all memoirs should be Things I Remember . . . and Things I Think I Remember."[1] Second, autobiographies and memoirs are often self-serving. As mentioned, in creating these accounts, politicians and other public leaders may have been anxious to secure their own place in history. Certain episodes in their lives may therefore be given more prominence than they deserve, as well as a highly favorable interpretation, while others, possibly less flattering, may be slighted, distorted, or ignored altogether. The same applies to the descriptions of the various other persons who are discussed in these accounts. This by no means renders memoirs or autobiographies worthless as source materials. Among other things, they provide invaluable insights into the personalities of leading figures. As with all source materials, however, the historian must begin by asking the purpose for which they were written or published, and then proceed with an appropriate measure of caution and skepticism.

A skeptical approach is also in order when considering materials like the published letters and diaries of public figures. These sources are perhaps more trustworthy in one respect, since they are contemporary with the events and not subject to the corrosive effects of time on memory. Even in this case, however, we must consider the author's motives, ignorance, or capacity for self-deception. Moreover, published source materials are frequently only a selection, and sometimes quite a small one, of the total body of a person's writings. We must therefore take into account the built-in bias of the selecting or editing process. How representative of the whole are the documents that are published? Did a favorably disposed editor (perhaps a member of the

---

[1]   Arthur M. Schlesinger Jr., *A Life in the Twentieth Century: Innocent Beginnings, 1917–1950* (Boston, MA: Houghton Mifflin, 2000), xiii.

family) suppress unflattering material? Even the most professional and even-handed editor must make painful choices about what materials to leave out. This is why historians always consult the largest and best edited collection of primary sources available, assuming of course that they do not have access to manuscript sources.

Somewhat different considerations apply to those written primary sources that are particularly valued by social historians. The development of interest in "history from below" has encouraged the finding and publication of the writings of ordinary people, who presumably never dreamed that their words would be published. The chance survival and later publication of the diary of an American pioneer woman or of the letters of a soldier in the Crimean War can vividly illuminate the lives and experiences of ordinary people. This does not mean, of course, that such documents can be accepted uncritically. While their authors were no doubt blissfully unconcerned about the opinion of posterity, their writings can be expected to reflect the normal human biases and blind spots. These "shortcomings" need not necessarily get in the way of our understanding; they may even be precisely the sort of thing we are looking for.

Let us now turn to primary-source materials like newspapers, magazines, and official reports of government or private institutions. Not only were these intended from the outset to be made public, but in many cases they were designed to influence public opinion. This is certainly the case with newspapers, whose editorial policies must be taken into account. Thus, to accept a newspaper account of one of the Lincoln–Douglas debates without considering the paper's political orientation would be a major critical lapse. Even if an article displayed no detectable bias, we would have to consider the problems inherent in relying upon a single reporter's account of an event: his vantage point, his ability to hear all that was said from the podium, the reactions of those in the crowd who were closest to him, and so on. Diligent historians assemble as many such accounts as they can, treating each of them critically, sorting out obvious biases and errors, and fashioning as accurate a reconstruction as possible.

We must approach other kinds of print media in much the same way. Magazines, journals, and pamphlets all offer a vast storehouse of facts as well as of prejudices. Like newspapers, they can reveal a great deal that the authors and editors never intended. Popular literature, sheet music, sermons, and plays can also tell us much about a society's common, unexamined assumptions. Consider the value of sources like these for, say, investigating nineteenth-century American attitudes toward gender roles or racial stereotyping. It is, however, necessary to read such material in two quite different ways. On the one hand, the historian must try to see the material as contemporaries did – an approach that requires both knowledge of the period and empathy for its people. Simultaneously, the material must be viewed through the critical, dispassionate eyes of a modern scholar who is posing questions that nineteenth-century people could not or did not ask.

There is an enormous variety and range of primary sources, only a few of which have been mentioned. When undertaking a research paper on a particular topic, it is well worth your time to consider in the first place *all* the types of sources you might use. A little investigation and imagination may lead you to use different sources from those employed by any previous scholar who has researched the same topic. Or they may enable you to approach the sources from an entirely new perspective. Conversely, if you are in the midst of trying to select a good topic, an awareness of the range of sources available to you might point you toward a highly interesting one, which otherwise you might not have considered.

Secondary Works

Secondary works or sources come in a great variety as well – from multivolume works of collective scholarship to short essays, from general histories to the most specialized monographs. Next we will consider some of the different forms that written histories can take: books, essays, and articles.

Books

Books are such a universal and commonplace feature of academic life that students seldom ponder about their diversity or unique structures. We can begin our consideration of the diversity of the types of history books from the breadth or narrowness of their subject. The extremes would be a textbook on the history of the world from the advent of human life to the present, and a study of a single individual or small community over a short span of time. In between these extremes are histories of such entities as civilizations, regions, nation-states, or social classes. Moreover, the approach can be political, social, economic, cultural, or some combination thereof; the style can be narrative or analytical, and the focus can be on individuals or on social aggregates. Finally, the tone can be "popular" or "scholarly" – that is, it may be calculated to appeal to a wide, nonprofessional readership or it may bristle with footnotes, statistics, and closely reasoned analysis designed to impress the author's scholarly peers.

Another method of distinguishing between history books is to ask whether they are based chiefly on primary or on secondary sources. As a rule, the broader the topic, the more the author relies on secondary works. Thus a book entitled *A History of the World* (or even *A History of the United States*) will probably not list many primary sources in its bibliography. You can see this for yourself by examining the bibliographies of one of the textbooks you have used (or are using) in a history survey course. Notice that the author's or authors' (many textbooks have multiple authors) account is fashioned out of the more specialized studies of other historians. New editions of texts are issued not only to bring the story up to the present, but to revise it in light of the most recent scholarship. In this way the fruits of the latest scholarship enter the general survey texts, and hence the classroom.

Survey textbooks and other general accounts are sometimes referred to as works of synthesis, because they synthesize or bring together the more specialized works of others. Those specialized works, especially when fairly narrow in scope and based on primary sources, are called monographs. Some monographs are simply detailed narrative accounts of particular subjects, but others attempt to break fresh interpretive ground and are thus important vehicles for historical revisionism. This does not mean, however, that works of synthesis cannot offer revisionist interpretations, for many of the most important revisionist works are those that offer fresh ways of interpreting the recent secondary literature. Also, this discussion of monographs and works of synthesis might imply a sharper barrier between them than in fact exists. Many history books, having elements of both synthesis and specialization, cannot be so tidily classified. Furthermore, the author of even the narrowest monograph is expected to take fully into account existing scholarship on the topic, that is, to place his or her analysis within a historiographic frame of reference.

Historians need and depend upon the contributions of other scholars, and many works of history are jointly written. In some cases two or more scholars may work closely together, both in doing the research and in writing the results. More commonly a general editor will coordinate the efforts of a team of historians, each of whom is given primary responsibility for a portion of the whole. A couple of examples are *The Oxford History of England* and *The Cambridge History of Islam*, both of them sponsored by large university presses. Other "joint" projects are published under the auspices of organizations like the United Nations – for example the UNESCO-sponsored *General History of Africa*. Collective authorship can be an effective means of attaining a degree of expertise beyond the reach of a single author. There is also a significant saving of time involved, though large joint projects have their own pitfalls, delays, and frustrations, which sorely test the skill and patience of general editors.

Whether scholarly monographs or survey texts, all history books have structural similarities that are important to note, especially when you are trying to determine quickly the approach, interpretation, and scope of a particular volume. The proper approach to your reading will be taken up in greater detail in Chapter 4, but a few pointers are in order here. A book's title will usually be descriptive of its scope, but the subtitle (if there is one) will usually tell you more. Recall the psychobiography of Jefferson by Fawn Brodie discussed in Chapter 1. The title itself,

Thomas Jefferson, indicates nothing more than that it is a biography. But the subtitle, *An Intimate History*, gives you a strong clue that this is not a standard political biography of Jefferson the public figure. If you look at the chapter headings in the table of contents and read the introduction, the approach and scope of the work should become clear. Also, a look at the index will let you preview a book quickly for the desired information.

Essays

An essay (sometimes simply called a "chapter") is a short, self-contained study, usually bound with similar pieces in book form. Like a book, an essay can be narrow or broad in scope, based on primary or secondary sources, and chiefly narrative or assertively interpretive. But its shorter span makes the essay a versatile and effective literary form for historians, as it is for scholars in the other humanities. Usually essays by various authors writing on different aspects of the same general topic or in the same field are combined into a single work with a revealing title such as *Essays in Business History*. The range of essays in such a volume might be very wide, from, say, an analysis of merchant enterprise in fourteenth-century Florence to a study of the start-up of high-tech industries in California.

Sometimes the essays will have been published previously, perhaps in a different form, for instance as an article in a scholarly journal. Often the earlier articles and essays of eminent historians will be gathered together and published. Sometimes each member of a group of historians who were trained by, or highly admire, the same scholar will contribute an essay to a book published in the mentor's honor, usually on the occasion of that person's retirement. Such a collection is called a *Festschrift*, a German word designating a presentation volume of essays dedicated to someone.[2]

[2] An example is Robert Robson, ed., *Ideas and Institutions of Victorian Britain: Essays in Honour of George Kitson Clark* (London: Bell & Sons, 1967). The title of this book gives no clue as to the specialized essays it contains. For this reason essays are sometimes called the "hidden literature." How to find this "hidden literature" will be one of our concerns in the next chapter.

Articles

Similar to essays in structure, length, and purpose, scholarly articles form an even more important segment of the body of secondary works. They are published in scholarly periodicals or journals, of which there is an enormous variety. Articles are often the format in which historians (and others) launch new interpretations. The revisionist process would be greatly retarded if scholarly journals were not able to publish and disseminate historical findings. For you, the student researcher, to ignore articles and to confine your attention to books alone would be to miss much of the freshest and most exciting literature on your subject. An appreciation of this large and diverse body of scholarship requires some understanding of the journals themselves – which, in turn, will lead us to a consideration of the structure of the historical profession.

Usually a periodical publication in which scholarly articles are published is called a journal. The term "magazine" should, in most cases, be confined to those periodicals of a more popular bent, such as *Newsweek* or the *Atlantic Monthly*. There are a few historical periodicals, like the British publication *History Today*, that have a popular magazine format, with short, amply illustrated articles meant to appeal to a wider readership. For the most part, however, historical journals are designed for a professional readership and feature lengthy, detailed articles, some of which can be daunting to the nonspecialist. But this should not intimidate the undergraduate researcher; a history student who is properly launched on a particular topic should find most of the scholarly articles on his or her topic both readable and stimulating.

Many historical journals are published by associations of historians, the costs of publication being defrayed in part by membership subscriptions. In the United States, one of the leading historical journals is the *American Historical Review*, the official organ of the American Historical Association (AHA). The AHA is the major "umbrella" organization for historians in the United States; its thousands of members include historians of almost every conceivable specialization or field of interest. Accordingly, the *American Historical Review* does not specialize in any one historical field. In each of its five annual issues one might find articles on such diverse topics as modern Europe, Tang Dynasty China, Hellenistic Egypt, and colonial America. Methodologically, the many articles represent all approaches to the past. Similarly, the hundreds of pages of book reviews that appear in each issue of this journal cover titles in all fields of history. Book reviews play a vitally important role in the evaluation and analysis of historical works. They are part of the elaborate apparatus by which new views are subjected to close critical scrutiny – in history as in other disciplines.

The *American Historical Review* is notable not just for its size and importance, but also because it is atypical of historical journals, the great majority of which have some kind of special focus. For example, The *Journal of American History* is published by the Organization of American Historians (OAH), whose members' primary interest is the history of the United States. This journal, as its name suggests, publishes articles and book reviews in the field of American history. The scope of many other journals is defined by their titles: *The Journal of Modern History*, *The Journal of African Studies*, *The Journal of Contemporary History*, and *Greek, Roman and Byzantine Studies*. Some specialize not in chronological periods or geographical areas, but in methodological approaches; such are *The Journal of Social History* and *The International Journal of Psychohistory*. Most journals are produced under the auspices of some professional organization. The North American Conference on British Studies, for example, supports the publication of *The Journal of British Studies*.

Many journals have a narrow focus. Those on local history are a prime example, and there is a great abundance of such publications in the United States. State historical societies and those devoted to the history of cities or other localities publish their own journals, which researchers ignore at their peril. Many important revisionist interpretations are produced in the form of article-length studies published in local history journals.

Local studies are not only important in and of themselves, but they also offer a valuable means of validating or refuting general historical hypotheses. Any assertion about a society's characteristics can be tested by examining particular localities in great detail. How, for example, would you attempt to test the claim that there was a high degree of social mobility in nineteenth-century America? Since searching for an answer to this question involves data that must be tracked over successive generations – the analysis of massive amounts of occupational data from the US Census as well as plenty of other material – a local study is often the most feasible procedure. One town's records would be much easier to decipher than those of the nation. Obviously, no single study of any single town could sustain or overturn the general hypothesis, but a number of such investigations might. Local studies, therefore, can and do contribute to an ever-emerging picture of regional or national history. Sometimes they serve the important purpose of pointing out significant differences among states, regions, or localities.

Dissertations and conference papers

Turning from those secondary sources that are readily accessible in published form – such as books, essays, and articles – let us consider now two other forms in which new findings are presented: scholarly dissertations and conference papers. A Doctorate of Philosophy (PhD) is the highest academic degree in history, and its completion requires the writing of a scholarly dissertation, usually on a rather narrow topic, on the basis of intensive research on primary sources. The granting of a PhD in history follows a committee of historians' certifying that the candidate's dissertation meets the standards of the profession. A dissertation is expected to demonstrate its author's critical acumen, writing abilities, and knowledge of the relevant primary and secondary sources. Dissertations are also usually expected to offer original analyses and interpretations. They can, therefore, be important works of new scholarship, and even of revisionist interpretation. Some are published subsequently as books; others will be substantially revised before ultimately being published or will eventually appear, after some modification, as journal articles. Even in their unrevised form, recent dissertations can be important tools for researchers. Not only do they offer new interpretations, but their bibliographies are particularly apt to be up to date and are therefore excellent guides to the topic's sources.[3]

Conference papers, delivered by historians to their peers at scholarly conferences (often the meetings of organizations like the AHA), might be described as the "cutting edge" of new scholarship. In many cases, this is the initial form in which the results of a historian's findings are made public and subjected to scrutiny and criticism. Often on the basis of the criticism received at a conference, a historian will revise his or her work before submitting it for publication. Typically, a conference paper is presented as part of a panel discussion that will hear and consider two or three papers on similar topics. After an introduction from the scholar chairing the panel, each presenter will read his or her work. After the papers have been read aloud (each requiring twenty minutes or so), a commentary on the papers is given by one of the panel's scholarly experts in the field. Sometimes printed or online versions of the papers are made available to prospective members of the audience beforehand, so they come to the session already familiar with the presenter's arguments. After all the papers have been read, or sometimes after each paper, the commentator offers criticism, advice, and often the delineation of some themes or threads that tie the papers together. At this point the audience is free to question, challenge, help refine, or offer counterinterpretations to points made in the papers. This can be a highly stimulating, albeit sometimes acrimonious, exchange, but it is one of the principal means by which new views are expressed and modified prior to publication.

---

[3] A bound copy of each dissertation is available in the library of the university granting the PhD, and often an extra copy is available through the interlibrary loan system. For those wishing to acquire their own copy, dissertations are available on microfilm and can be purchased from University Microfilms corporations.

To get some idea of how this process operates, let us consider the largest historical conference of them all: the annual meeting of the AHA. Held over a four-day period, the AHA's annual meeting is a vast smorgasbord of offerings, with clusters of panels running simultaneously. At the January 2012 meeting in Chicago, for example, there were more than 250 panels and roundtables on everything – from "The varieties of religious conflict in the Middle Ages" to "Cold War kids: The ideologies of punk in the East and the West."[4] Each of the panels tends to attract for its audience specialists in the particular field, though many participants find it stimulating to attend at least a few panels well outside their primary areas of interest.

In addition to the panels, the annual meeting is an occasion for publishers of scholarly books in history to display their wares. This is an important source of information for historians about the latest publications in the field. There are also numerous opportunities for social and intellectual exchanges during conferences: individual encounters, receptions, and the luncheons of the many historical societies affiliated to the AHA. It is these affiliated societies (subgroups of the AHA's membership) that are apt to be the primary focus of most historians' professional involvement. Many, if not most, of these smaller groups also hold regular meetings and conferences independently of the AHA meeting. Like the specialized journals that cater to particular fields, the hundreds of historical societies are organized along geographic, cultural, chronological, or methodological lines. Such groups as the Medieval Academy of America, the American Conference on Irish Studies, the Society for the History of Technology, and the World History Association represent crucial parts of the infrastructure of the historical profession.

This account of the basic organizational features of the profession is introduced in order to give some sense of the dynamic and cooperative character of modern scholarship. It is important for you to realize that most books and articles you will encoun-

---

[4] American Historical Association, *Program of the 126th Annual Meeting, January 5–8, 2012* (Washington, DC: American Historical Association, 2011).

ter were not written by "ivory tower" types working in complete isolation, but by men and women (many still in their twenties and from all parts of the nation and of the world) developing and refining their views in relation to the methods and criticisms of others. This is what we mean when we describe the historical profession, or some segment of it, as a "community of scholars."

But now it is time to go to the sources. In the next chapter we will explore the various methods of finding the works you will need to research your topic.

3

Finding Your Sources
The Online Library Catalog and Beyond

A child who asks for an item of general information will often be told to "look it up." This response, though it may sometimes stem from an unwillingness to admit ignorance, is an educationally sound one. Its tendency is to make the child a self-directed learner and to prompt him or her to develop basic research skills. Even though the information found in a children's encyclopedia or from a basic search on the internet is decidedly limited, the lesson imparted is invaluable: that a storehouse of accumulated information is literally at one's fingertips. Beyond the home, the maturing student discovers the richer offerings of community and school libraries, which, together with increasing sophistication in the use of the computer, nourish the spirit of inquiry. Admission to college brings with it the highest stage of access to the written word in the form of the university library, the resources of which are usually more voluminous and varied than anything encountered previously. It also brings a much richer array of computer resources than those available in the home or at school – even in high school.

Going to the Sources: A Guide to Historical Research and Writing, Fifth Edition.
Anthony Brundage.
© 2013 John Wiley & Sons, Ltd. Published 2013 by John Wiley & Sons, Ltd.

In spite of the impressiveness of most campus libraries, many students remain unaware of the great diversity of materials and services they offer. Nor are they usually well grounded in navigating this complex array. Typical writing assignments, such as term papers and book reviews, rarely require anything more than a few books from the library stacks. The procedure is simple and straightforward. Find some titles in the library catalog, jot down the call numbers (or shelf numbers), go to the shelves and collect them, and check them out. Now you can mine the selected volumes for information, including perhaps a few choice quotations. If you need additional material on a particular person or historical incident, you can consult one of the large and authoritative encyclopedias in the library's reference room. These days students are also apt to resort to the internet, perhaps even beginning their research there (some, alas, may end it there as well). Having filled up some note cards or notebooks during this process, the student uses them to write the paper. At this point many students think that their work in the library is done, at least until the next such assignment.

The procedure just outlined may serve well enough for the requirements of some lower division survey courses. Its shortcomings become painfully obvious, however, as soon as one turns to more advanced coursework. Therefore a few of the notable deficiencies of this time-honored yet short-sighted method of undergraduate research should be considered. First, it is probably directed at only one or two of the several subject headings or keywords through which books on the topic might be found. Second, by being confined to the books the university library happens to possess, it ignores a vast and efficient interlibrary loan network, which can obtain most published works on any topic within a couple of weeks. Third, it makes no attempt to access scholarly journals, with their wealth of information and new interpretations. It also ignores potentially valuable essays (or "chapters") on the topic that will not come up in a simple catalog search. Finally, it does not take into account the great variety of more specialized reference works that will prove helpful. These deficiencies can be corrected by learning about several vital library services often overlooked or underutilized by students: reference materials, periodicals, and the interlibrary loan system.

The Online Library Catalog

Before examining these facilities, however, we should take a look back at a part of the library that students already know (or think they know) how to use well: the Online Library Catalog. Often called OPAC (Online Public Access Catalog), this computerized system offers numerous benefits over the old card catalog. After no more than the few minutes required to learn the basics of the terminal, one can conduct a complete search from a single location. Moreover, terminals are increasingly found in convenient locations throughout the library, and even on other parts of the campus. Most convenient of all, you can carry out an online catalog search from your own computer. Finally, in addition to listing the books and periodicals in your library, OPAC is the gateway to a large array of electronic resources.

Before embarking upon this electronic odyssey, it is important to know the object of the search. The selection and refinement of your topic is of course a critical matter. It may be assigned by your instructor, but usually the student is expected to develop his or her own topic, often within some defined parameters. Consultation with your instructor regarding the feasibility of your intended topic is always a good idea, but it should be realized that your topic will probably change during the course of your research. Usually the change will be in the direction of limiting or pruning, since on many occasions the original topic is found to be overly broad. If, for example, your first idea was to write about nineteenth-century imperialism, you would have quickly discovered (or been told) that this was far too vast a subject. Seeking to limit it, you might have chosen British imperialism, German imperialism, or perhaps "the scramble for Africa." These topics proving in turn unmanageable, you might have tried narrowing chronologically, geographically, or topically: say, to "German involvement in East Africa, 1884–98," or "Cecil Rhodes and the expansion of the British Empire in South Africa, 1890–1902." However, delimiting your topic in this fashion requires that you already know something about imperialism or that you have started your research by reading some general work on the subject.

Subject Headings, Keywords, and Title Words

In the pre-computer age, researchers were confined to looking for book titles through a card system in which items were arranged by author, title, and subject. A researcher interested in a particular topic was heavily dependent upon the subject headings catalog, and typically spent a good deal of time determining what subject headings to use. Consulting the *Library of Congress Subject Headings*, a multivolume reference work, facilitated the process; but one always experienced considerable guesswork and frustration. While modern-day researchers should not expect instant results, the computer has made the location process much faster and easier. In OPAC the titles are arranged not only under the categories of "author," "title," and "subject," but also under "title words" (or "words in title") and under "keywords." In using the latter two categories you do not need to know the subject headings before you start searching. It is often advisable to start with this method, as in many cases it will prove speedier; but, before considering how to search by title words or keywords, let us examine the more conventional approach using author, title, and subject headings.

You may start your research knowing that you want to consult certain works that your instructor has mentioned or that you have seen referenced in your textbooks. The author and the title entries will provide the call numbers for these works, and the volumes can be garnered from the stacks, assuming of course that they are part of the library's holdings. Use of the "subject" entries, however, requires more care and thought. Under which subject headings should you look? Several subject headings, perhaps as many as a dozen, will yield useful titles, but it is up to you to determine which one(s) to look under. This is where it becomes important to spend some time analyzing your topic, thinking about the various subjects of which it forms a part. After all, very few of the books in your final bibliography will focus precisely on your topic.

Fortunately the determination of subject headings is not a matter of guesswork. After spending a few minutes thinking about and jotting down some possible subject headings, you can always consult the above-mentioned *Library of Congress Subject Headings*. These reference volumes will allow you to discover what exact subject headings have been established in the classification system. With this information you can then go back to perusing the subject entries in the catalog and continue your search.

Now you will almost certainly be looking through a rather disparate range of subject headings. For example, if your topic is German imperialism in Africa, a couple of useful subject headings turn out to be "Germany – Colonies – Africa" and "Germany – Colonies – History." As you begin to read some of the books on this topic, you might return to the subject catalog to search under the heading "Peters, Karl." This refers to the intrepid German explorer and empire builder whose career bulks as large in the history of German East Africa as that of Cecil Rhodes does in the history of British South Africa. It is an example of how a number of topics turn out to have significant biographical components. Important information on your topic would thus be found in a biography of Peters. The reverse is also true. Having a biographical topic like Cecil Rhodes might seem to simplify the process: just copy down the entries under "Rhodes, Cecil" and you are through. But here, too, there will be a number of headings – important information about and interpretations of Rhodes are contained in studies of South Africa in the late nineteenth century, in histories of Rhodesia, and in accounts of the background of the Boer War.

At this point you may be wondering if all this means that you must somehow manage to determine all the subject headings for your topic in order to compile a complete bibliography. The answer is no. Library cataloguers, in their infinite wisdom and mercy, have devised a useful system of cross-referencing for the great majority of entries in OPAC. Let's say that you had begun to research the history of women in the United States. You would have learned from the *Library of Congress Subject Headings* that one of the headings to use is "Women – United States – History." Entering this heading in the online catalog (you don't have to type the dashes, just the words), you would find a number of potentially useful titles, including one that we encountered in Chapter 1: June Sochen's *Herstory.*

AUTHOR	Sochen, June, 1937
TITLE	Herstory: a woman's view of American history/ June Sochen
PUBLISHER	New York: Alfred Pub. Co. [1974]
DESCRIPT	xiii, 448 p. : ill. ; 24 cm
NOTES	Includes bibliographies and index
SUBJECT	Women – United States – History.
	Minorities – United States.
	Women – United States – Social conditions.
	United States – Social conditions.
Books/4th floor	HQ1410 .S64 AVAILABLE
Books/4th floor	HQ1410 .S64 c. 2 AVAILABLE

While screen displays vary from one OPAC system to another, the following bibliographic information will be shown:

In addition to the title, author, call number, date and place of publication, and publisher, we are given other basic information: the book has 13 pages of front matter (note the Roman numeral xiii); 448 pages of text; and contains illustrations (note the "ill."), a bibliography, and an index. We can also see that this particular library has two copies of the book, neither of which is currently checked out. But it is the list of subject headings under which this volume is indexed that is of special interest to us. These are the four headings listed near the bottom of the screen. The first of them is the heading that was used to find this particular entry. The other three are headings under which Sochen's book can also be located, along with other works likely to be of interest to you. Get into the habit of jotting down the other subject headings (sometimes there is only one) from each catalog entry you look up. Most online catalog systems make it extremely easy to check the listing under the other subject headings, as there will be a link on the screen labeled something like "Show similar items" or "Show items with the same subject." When you select this, you can then choose whichever of the other subject headings you wish, and you will quickly see a somewhat different range of titles (not only books, but other sources such as DVDs, videos, CDs, and so on), some of which you may want to add to your bibliography.

Usually it is best to avoid starting with a "subject" search altogether and begin instead with a search by title words (sometimes called "words in title" or "words") or by keywords. The phrase *title words* is self-explanatory: it designates a search by any word that appears in the title or subtitle of a book. Keywords include words in subject headings as well as in titles. Let's say that you are working on a paper on the employment of women in the United States during World War II, and that you know that there is a book with "Rosie the Riveter" in the title – or simply think it likely those words might be in the title of a book. By choosing the "title words" option, you could type "rosie" and "riveter" to call up the volume (there are actually several books with these words in the title). Here is the entry for one useful-sounding book, with call number and location information omitted:

AUTHOR	Honey, Maureen, 1945
TITLE	Creating Rosie the Riveter: Class, Gender, and Propaganda during World War II / Maureen Honey
PUBLISHER	Amherst: University of Massachusetts Press, 1984
DESCRIPT	x, 251 p. : ill. ; 24 cm
NOTES	Includes index
	Bibliography: p. [241]–248

SUBJECT   Women – United States – History – 20th century.
Women in mass media – United States – History
– 20th century.
Women – Employment – United States – History
– 20th century.
World War, 1939–1945 – Women – United States.
Women – United States – Social conditions.

Now you have five valuable subject headings under which to search, though the third and the fourth seem to hold the most promise for a paper on your topic. You can now select the "Show similar items" from the menu; or, if the online catalog in your library doesn't have this feature, simply type in each of the subject headings you would like to use. The keywords function is an excellent means of jumpstarting a search on any topic, and it is usually possible to guess what words are likely to appear in the title of a book on any given topic.

Another way to employ a keyword or title word search to good effect is to think about possible titles of works with a somewhat wider scope than your topic. Very frequently such works will have lengthy chapters, or perhaps entire sections, devoted to your topic. Thus, staying with the example of research for a paper on women during World War II, in addition to using words such as "Rosie the Riveter" to lead you to titles on your subject, consider using words like "home front." Such a search will reveal a number of valuable works.[1]

Creating and Using a Research Bibliography

Another important habit to acquire early on in the game is developing complete bibliographic entries for all the titles that are

---

[1] For example Allan Winkler, *Home Front USA: America during World War II*, 2nd ed. (Wheeling, IL: Harlan Davidson, 2001).

obviously – or even potentially – of use to you in your research. You can either use 3 × 5 cards or write the entries in a notebook and transfer them to your computer at the end of the day. Many OPAC systems give you the option of e-mailing the information on library materials to yourself – a process that facilitates creating a bibliographic entry for each work on your computer. If you are searching from home or you have a laptop with you wherever you are, you can enter the items directly into your computer, always making sure to save and back up your bibliography file frequently. There are also bibliographic software programs that make it easy to search out titles, download them to your computer, and format them in any of a number of ways that you specify. If you are using a card, write the author's or editor's name on the top line (last name first) and the title, publication data (place, publisher, date), and call number below. Thus the above entry, if handwritten on a 3 × 5 card, would look like this:

Honey, Maureen

Creating Rosie the Riveter: Class, Gender, and Propaganda during World War II.

Amherst: University of Massachusetts Press, 1984.

HQ 1420

H66

1984

When you enter titles into a computer, hit the "Return" key only when you are moving on to the next book, article, or essay. That way you can use the sort or alphabetizing function of your word-processing application, which will instantly arrange your entries alphabetically, by authors' last names. Thus the above entry should be entered into a computer as follows:

> Honey, Maureen. *Creating Rosie the Riveter: Class, Gender, and Propaganda during World War II.* Amherst: University of Massachusetts Press, 1984.

Note that, on the handwritten card, the title of the book is underlined, which is the convention for showing items that will be italicized in print. When you enter the same information in the computer, there is no point in underlining – just use the italicizing function that every word-processing application contains. Also, in making computer entries, use the paragraph formatting function of your word processor for indenting the second and subsequent lines rather than the Tab key. Using tabs will produce problems if you later change font size or margins, or if you make any changes in wording. As you build up your bibliography file, keep it alphabetized, so that you can tell at a glance if you already have an entry on a particular book. Even if you are working directly from an alphabetized computer bibliographic file, you should always have a hard copy of it on hand. You will probably also find it useful to make brief notations, on your bibliography cards or computer hard copy, on such matters as the particular library in which you found the book and whether you have already read or at least looked at it; brief annotations on its contents will also prove helpful.

Once your project is launched, always have your card file (or the hard copy of your computerized bibliography file) with you when you enter the library, or when you go online for further research. As you access the stacks using the catalog, new titles will loom into view frequently. One of the ways this happens may already be familiar to you – it is called "shelf browsing." This entails simply looking at the volumes adjacent to those books you have gone to the stacks to fetch; some of your target book's neighbors are almost certain to prove valuable. Many online systems have a menu option that lets you "shelf browse" electronically. Another important method of adding titles to your bibliography is mining the bibliographies of the books you already have found. As soon as you get your hands on a new volume, examine its bibliography for other sources you do not know about yet. One of the advantages of this method is that it will let you identify wanted titles that your library does not have among its holdings, many of which can then be obtained through interlibrary loan or by going to another library.

Published Bibliographies

Another very effective means of finding useful titles is to consult published bibliographies available in book, article, or essay form. Sometimes good bibliographies on your topic are available on the internet. It may indeed be advisable to begin your search in this fashion. I have deferred discussing this resource until now because I think it essential to start with some knowledge of the organization of the library catalog. Also, consulting a published bibliography on your topic at the outset might tend to shortcircuit your search and thus to interfere with learning some basic research procedures. Bear in mind, too, that, even if you find a comprehensive published bibliography exactly on your topic, it is not going to include any titles published after it went to press, which is often a year or more prior to its publication date. Thus, even with a recently published bibliography in hand, you still must search elsewhere in order to find the most recent books, articles, and essays on your topic. Don't assume, either, that a bibliography you find online contains the latest materials; quite apart from questions of quality (a particular concern with internet resources), it may have been a considerable time since that website was created or updated.

In addition to those scholars who write histories or edit primary-source materials, others provide a most valuable service by collecting and publishing bibliographies on various subjects. These are intended as guides for researchers and provide a list of books and articles on a given subject, with entries often arranged under subtopics and sometimes annotated. (Annotations are the editor's comments and indicate something about the scope and usefulness of each entry.) When these research guides are written as essays rather than presented simply as lists of titles, they are called bibliographic essays.

Bibliographies can be located in a number of ways. The subject index of the catalog is one such method. When you have discovered an appropriate heading for your topic, look at the headings immediately following it to see if there is one with the word "Bibliography" added. It will be recalled that, for research on the history of American women, one of the key headings is "Women – United States – History." Immediately following is the subject heading "Women – United States – History – Bibliography." Here will be found the titles of a number of valuable bibliographies on this topic or on some portion of it. An example is Jill K. Conway, *The Female Experience in Eighteenth- and Nineteenth-Century America: A Guide to the History of American Women* (New York: Garland, 1982). Conway's bibliography lists the titles of thousands of books, articles, and collections of primary sources on various facets of the history of American women. Remember, however, that a great deal has been published on this topic since the appearance of this bibliography, so you still need to undertake a full search using the methods described in this chapter. Also, if you have already decided on a narrower period for which you want to research American women's history, you should check to see if there is a more focused bibliography, such as Theresa McDevitt's *Women and the American Civil War: An Annotated Bibliography* (Westport, CT: Praeger, 2003). The main point is that, whenever you look up something in the subject headings in OPAC, it's a good idea to check to see if there is also a bibliography heading for your topic. The same holds true for finding primary sources. If there are published sources for your topic in the library, there will be a heading in the subject index with the word "Sources" added. Look, for example, under the heading "Women – United States – History – Sources."

In the reference room of your library there are other ways to access bibliographies. There are even several good "bibliographies of bibliographies," which list bibliographies in all fields. A valuable one for historical researchers is Robert Balay, ed., *Guide to Reference Books*, 11th ed. (Chicago: American Library Association, 1996). By looking up the entries under history and the appropriate subheading, you will find references to bibliographic works on your topic or on the field of history of which your topic is a part. One particularly valuable bibliographic reference tool for historical researchers in all fields is Mary Beth Norton, ed., *The*

American Historical Association's *Guide to Historical Literature* (New York: Oxford University Press, 1995).

A good method of finding relevant titles that your library may not have is to consult the subject index of *Books in Print*, a multivolume reference work that is frequently updated and is also available online. Whether you use the electronic or the printed form of *Books in Print*, it is always a good idea to check every few weeks to see if any new items have been added under your subject's heading. The practice of examining the latest printed supplements or the computerized databases to check for additions to the body of scholarship on your topic applies as well to the other indexes and abstracts, which we will now consider – those that provide access to articles and book reviews in scholarly journals, and also to essays in books.

Printed and Electronic Indexes and Abstracts

In the last chapter we saw the importance of scholarly journals in the process of historical revisionism. Scholarly articles are not mere adjuncts to books; they are efficient vehicles for presenting various kinds of special studies, as well as the initial form in which historians often challenge existing interpretations. It is therefore vitally important to find and read the relevant periodical literature. There are a number of indexing and abstracting resources available online for this purpose; some will also lead you to additional book titles, as well as to book reviews. Most of them are published quarterly and bound into volumes at the end of each year, along with a comprehensive index of the year's issues. Some publications offer five- or ten-year indexes to facilitate research. Whether you are using the online database or the published index, when you first consult each of these reference works, spend a few minutes acquainting yourself with their internal organization and determine which subject headings are used for your topic. If you are using an online database, check (by the publication dates of your sources) to see how far back in time it goes; it may index only materials published in the last ten years or so. If this is the case, you will have to use the published form of the index if you need to locate older materials. When using the published index, start with the most recent date and work your way backward in time.

How far back in time you go depends upon your topic, the kind of paper you are preparing to write, and the guidelines set by your instructor. Keep in mind that, unlike in the sciences, in engineering, or in medicine, the older literature in the field of history does not necessarily become "obsolete." Furthermore, when preparing a historiographic essay – which is, after all, a history of historical writing on your topic – you will have to consider older titles as well as the more recent ones. The indexes, abstracts, and other finding aids discussed in the following pages are also, for convenience, listed in Appendices A and B. These can function as handy checklists when you are carrying out your research on a particular topic.

It is obviously desirable to find full text articles online whenever possible, as this represents a significant saving of time over going to the stacks for printed articles or sending off requests for them through interlibrary loan. The single most useful database for historical researchers looking for relevant periodical literature is JSTOR. Most of the major English-speaking historical journals are covered in JSTOR, and the full text of articles going back to the beginning of each publication is available online (in the case of the *American Historical Review*, for example, beginning in 1895). What is not available on JSTOR are the most recent issues of a journal. Thus there is a gap, ranging from one to five years and going back from the most recent printed copy of the journal. That gap is filled admirably by another database, Humanities Full Text. This is one of many indexes published by the W. W. Wilson Company, and, depending upon the electronic set-up in your library, it may be available (back to a certain point in time) as part of the WilsonWeb database. Be sure to prepare a card or computer entry for each article you find, including all the essential bibliographic information: author, title, name of journal, volume, date, and page numbers. If, for example, you were writing a paper on King Louis XIV of France, you would find in both databases a full text article from Volume 18 of *French Histori-cal Studies*. A card on this item would read as follows:

Smith, Jay M.

"'Our sovereign's gaze': Kings, nobles, and state formation in seventeenth-century France." French Historical Studies 18.2 (1993): 396–415.

The example above is of a handwritten card. The volume number of *French Historical Studies* in which this article appears is 18; the inclusive page numbers of the article are 396 to 415. Note that abbreviations like "vol." (for volume), or even "pp." (for pages) are often not used, especially in standard references, or for inter-nal purposes. But do bear in mind that this specification can be useful and is sometimes even required – not only as a sty-listic feature, but in more complex kinds of material, where the number could indicate something quite different from page: item number (for example in collections of fragments, inscrip-tions, or coins); folium of an early modern editio princeps (as in standard references to Plato, Aristotle, and so on); or even more familiar categories like column, chapter, or section. This entry in your computer, in the same format as the final printed bibli-ography at the end of your completed paper, and substituting italicizing for underlining, would look like this:

Smith, Jay M. "'Our sovereign's gaze': Kings, nobles, and state forma-tion in seventeenth-century France." *French Historical Studies* 18.2 (1993): 396–415.

A number of more specialized indexes to periodical literature may be of interest to you, depending on your topic. For any topic in British or European history, the *British Humanities Index* (*BHI*) is apt to prove useful. The *Hispanic American Periodicals Index* (*HAPI*) is invaluable for any facet of Latin American history or the history of Hispanics in the United States. Those researching any aspect of the history of law will want to consult the *Index to Legal Periodicals*. The law journals indexed there are, for the most part, not found in other indexes. (Some of the articles in law journals are of a historical character and are important vehicles for launching revisionist interpretations.) Other indexes that may prove valuable to historical researchers are the *Biography Index*, the *Art Index*, the *Music Index*, and *Index Medicus*.

Databases that do not offer full text retrieval sometimes give details about the content of the articles; these details are referred to as abstracts. The organization of the material is very similar to that of indexes, which give only the bibliographic particulars; but in databases more information is provided – after each entry there is a description of the scope and contents of the article. This does not mean, however, that you can ignore the more bare-bones indexes and go straight to the ones that offer abstracts. A quite different range of scholarly journals is covered in the abstracts, and the most widely available set of abstracts for European and world history covers only the period from the Renaissance to the present. Even for modern history you would miss some important articles, since some of the journals covered by the more restrictive indexes are not covered by those that provide abstracts. These are simply some of the quirks in the organization of material for historical research.

For our purposes, the two databases that are most important for abstracts are *Historical Abstracts* and *America: History and Life*.[2] The first is for world history and for European history from the Renaissance to the present, while the latter is concerned with American history. Like other indexes, these abstracts are available both in printed and in electronic form. If your library has them in the latter form, remember to check to see how far back it goes. The structure and arrangement of the printed abstracts are

[2] *Dissertation Abstracts International* is also very useful, but, since it is cross-indexed in both *Historical Abstracts* and *America: History and Life*, it is not necessary to search through it directly. If you come across an entry, either in *Historical Abstracts* or in *America: History and Life*, with the code DAI affixed, copy down the volume and abstract number, then look it up in *Dissertation Abstracts International*. Many dissertations can be ordered on interlibrary loan.

somewhat different from those found in the other indexes, so spend a little time to orient yourself before beginning your search. You will find that each abstract collection is organized into several parts: article abstracts and citations; an index to book reviews; a bibliography of books, articles, and dissertations; and an annual index. In the electronic form the categories are combined in the index, and you can limit your search by choosing to go by document type (book, article, etc.), by time period, or by other categories. When you call up a screen, it will indicate whether the item is a book, an article, a dissertation, or a book review. The subject headings will differ from those encountered so far, because now you are dealing exclusively with historical materials. Thus, for example, you will find no heading with "History" appended to it. Nor will "United States" be added to subject headings in *America: History and Life*.

Also note the much greater number of journals listed in the abstracts. Unlike the indexes, the abstracts comprise many journals of local history. In *America: History and Life*, for example, you will see a very large number of publications concerned with state and local history, like the *Utah Historical Quarterly*, the *Pennsylvania Magazine of Biography and History*, the *Southern California Quarterly*, and *Chicago History*. You might think that these journals would be of little use to you unless your topic were somehow related to the state or city in question. But remember from our discussion of secondary works in Chapter 2 that important revisionist scholarship often appears in the form of local studies. Thus, if you were writing about the Freedmen's Bureau, this subject heading in *America: History and Life* would lead you to the abstract of an article by James Stealey that bears the title of "The Freedmen's Bureau in West Virginia" and was published in the journal *West Virginia History*. The bibliographic information and the accompanying abstract are displayed in the following fashion:

17 A: 1135. Stealey, James Edmund III. THE FREEDMEN'S BUREAU IN WEST VIRGINIA. *West Virginia History* 1978 39(2–3): 99–142. During 1865–68 the Freedmen's Bureau was active in Berkeley and

Jefferson counties, West Virginia, where freedmen were a fifth of the population. The young army officers in charge were zealous for the blacks' welfare but did not have much success in protecting their legal rights. The establishment of schools met a mixed white reception, especially where the black attendance was large; the Bureau's most significant effort was in the founding of Storer College, a Negro normal school. Based on Freedmen's Bureau records and other primary and secondary sources; 216 notes. J. H. Broussard.

The information supplied here will help you decide whether to add this title to your bibliography. If your paper was on the educational activities of the Freedmen's Bureau, you certainly would want it. Note also that this is quite a lengthy article, it is based on research on the primary sources, and it has a large number of footnotes or endnotes. J. H. Broussard wrote the abstract. If you decide to use it, fill out a bibliography entry and submit an interlibrary loan request (unless, of course, your library has *West Virginia History* among its holdings). Note that the format of the abstract is a little different from the one you should use for making a bibliography card or computer entry. In your records the above item should be rendered as:

Stealey, James Edmund III. "The Freedmen's Bureau in West Virginia." *West Virginia History* 39 (1978): 99–142.

Following a widespread convention, article titles go in quotation marks and tend nowadays to be lowercased, while the name of a journal (*West Virginia History*) is always italicized (underlined on a handwritten bibliography card). The volume number is 39, the page numbers are 99 to 142. The issue number (2–3 in this example) is unnecessary for your own use.

Finding Scholarly Essays

The procedures just described should guide you efficiently to articles in the scholarly journals. But how does one find scholarly

essays (or chapters) that in books whose titles give little or no clue to the specialized nature of the essays they contain? This is the problem of the "hidden literature" referred to in Chapter 2. The answer is to consult that highly useful reference source, the *Essay and General Literature Index*. Organized like the other indexes and available both online and in print, it provides access to the titles of essays that appear in books. For example, if your topic is the economic aspect of decolonization in Africa, under the subject heading "Africa" in the *Essay and General Literature Index* you will find a reference to an essay by Jean Suret-Canale titled "From colonization to independence in French tropical Africa: The economic background," in a book titled *The Transfer of Power in Africa*. Deciding that this would definitely be useful, you proceed to fill out a bibliography card as follows:

Suret-Canale, Jean
"From colonization to independence in French tropical Africa: The economic back-
ground." In Prosser Gifford and William Roger Louis (eds.), The Transfer of Power
in Africa: Decolonization, 1940–1960, pp. 445–81. New Haven, CT: Yale University
Press, 1982.

This same item in your computerized bibliography is:

> Suret-Canale, Jean. "From colonization to independence in French tropical Africa: The economic background." In Prosser Gifford and William Roger Louis (eds.), *The Transfer of Power in Africa: Decolonization, 1940–1960*, pp. 445–81. New Haven, CT: Yale University Press, 1982.

Now proceed to look up the book in the library catalog to see if *The Transfer of Power in Africa* is in your library's collection. If not, you need to order this item through interlibrary loan. Be sure you request it by the title of the book, not of the essay, and that you list Prosser Gifford and William Roger Louis in the author's position, though they are in fact the editors of the volume.

Other Important Databases

In addition to the databases and published indexes described above, there are others that make available a huge array of titles of books, articles, essays, and conference papers, as well as newspaper articles and a variety of reference materials. One of the most valuable of them is WorldCat – the combined catalogued holdings of thousands of libraries, searchable by keywords as well as by subject headings, author, and title. This is an excellent means of finding books on your topic that your own university library does not have. In many cases you can submit your request electronically from the same screen on which you found the book, by using the "Order" command. This command sends a request to the interlibrary loan office in your library, which in turn orders the book for you. It is not necessary, by the way, for you to note where the needed volume is located – only that it exists. The staff in your interlibrary loan office (or document delivery, or whatever it is called on your campus) will order it, usually electronically, from the location from which delivery is apt to be the speediest. Because there is always some delay involved in procuring items through interlibrary loan, it is vitally important to get on to an early start with your bibliographic search.

One caveat about WorldCat: it is so enormous that simply using a basic keyword search will bring up thousands of titles of all kinds of materials – clearly an unmanageable situation. To avoid this, select the option "Advanced search" or "Expert search"; this allows you to limit your search according to such criteria as language, document type, year of publication, and so on. Another caveat is that not all of the books you find on WorldCat can be obtained through interlibrary loan. Some are in restricted circulation at the libraries that hold them.[3]

Another database especially useful for historical researchers is ArticleFirst. As with WorldCat, it's a good idea to use the "Advanced search" or "Expert search" option. As with WorldCat again, the item (in this case an article or a book review) can be requested electronically through interlibrary loan, by using the "Order" command at the bottom of the screen. Before submitting a request, however, doublecheck to make sure that your library does not have the item. In the case of an article or book review, this means checking to see if your library has not only the journal, but the specific volume number of the journal in which the needed item appears (many libraries have only certain volumes of any given periodical). There is a very handy "Lib" command at the bottom of the screen in ArticleFirst and World-Cat. This will display the libraries that have the item. More precisely, it will display an alphabetical listing of code letters for the libraries that have the item. Find out the code for your library and, if it does not appear on the screen, just submit an interlibrary loan request.

A few other good databases for historical researchers should be noted. One is OmniFile Full Text Mega, which, like Humanities Full Text and the *Essay and General Literature Index* (both discussed above), are part of the WilsonWeb cluster of databases. The names of some of these databases may give the impression that the articles you find in them will be full texts rather than just bibliographic citations. This is true in the case of many of the articles, but for others you will simply get the bibliographic citation for the items you seek. With the passage of time more and more materials will be available in full text form; but in the foreseeable future you will have to acquire most articles through the more traditional means already discussed. Two other valuable

---

[3]   Many universities belong to a regional consortium of libraries such as the Link Plus system in California, which have mutual borrowing privileges and a streamlined interlibrary loan system. This is frequently the most convenient and efficient way of obtaining books that are not among your library's holdings.

databases are Academic Search Elite and World History Full Text, which are, both, part of the EBSCO cluster of databases (the acronym stands for Elton B. Stephens Company). As with all databases, the interface will vary from library to library. In some cases databases will be listed directly in alphabetical fashion, while in others you will have to click on WilsonWeb (or on whatever cluster the database you need is included in).

Historical Research on the Internet

The internet has undergone extraordinary expansion in the last few years, and many websites are quite valuable to historical researchers. They offer an array of primary and secondary sources, along with archives of historical maps, photographs, and other images. A web address or URL ("uniform resource locator," previously "universal resource locator") usually begins with "http," which stands for "hypertext transfer protocol." When you find a particular site useful, you will no doubt want to return to it, so remember to bookmark it.

Since many websites are ephemeral while others frequently change their URLs, it would be pointless to list specific sites here. The important thing is to be effecient in searching for websites relevant to your topic. A number of good search engines are available; such are Google and Yahoo, which will lead you to useful material. The problem is assessing the importance of the many hits, perhaps hundreds, that a typical search on one of the search engines might yield. The internet is a vast, uncoordinated arena wherein good sites are generally outnumbered by those that are worthless, occasionally vicious, or focused on selling something – although the major search engines continue to improve. A few years ago an internet search for "Hitler" would have turned up a few really valuable hits buried among a host of sites organized by neo-Nazi cultists, sellers of Third Reich memorabilia, and Holocaust deniers. The junk sites are still out there, but, on the whole, the search engines do a much better job of placing the valuable sites near the top of their lists. Still, internet research requires that you choose your search terms with some care. You may need to try a number of alternatives before finding the right ones. When confronted with a large number of hits after even a careful search, try to make what critical assessments you can from the description of each site on the list. There are some very useful recent books on how to locate valuable websites and use them effectively, such as Andrew McMichael's *History on the Web*.[4]

There is certainly a rapidly expanding array of riches available to historical researchers on the internet. In spite of this abundance, however, the number of these online sources is still dwarfed by that of sources available in print, and this is likely to remain true for a long time. Think of the history sites on the internet as a valuable adjunct to printed sources and other media, not as a substitute for them.

Finding Useful Reference Materials

During the research for and the writing of any paper, it is necessary to look up certain key facts or dates and to acquire additional background information about a particular event or person. While a ready resort to Wikipedia is tempting and often fruitful, it should be observed that the quality of the articles varies considerably and that even the very good ones do not necessarily provide the kind of information you require. The reference rooms of a good library hold a great diversity of materials of interest to historians and student researchers, including encyclopedias (general and specialized), biographical dictionaries, historical atlases, chronologies, and official guides to various nations. Some of these items, especially the more general encyclopedias, are readily available online.[5] For the most part, however, the more special-

---

[4]   Andrew McMichael, *History on the Web: Using and Evaluating the Internet* (Wheeling, IL: Harlan Davidson, 2005).
[5]   An excellent gateway to a large range of such materials is at www.refdesk. com.

ized reference materials that you will require in your work are in printed form. Many of them will be available in the reference room of your library; others are shelved in the regular stacks. There are also some good published guides to reference materials.[6]

At an early stage of your research, you should reconnoiter the reference room, since there are important variations from library to library. For example, in some of them all the atlases will be found together, regardless of the part of the world or time period they cover. Maybe all the biographical materials will also be grouped together, without regard to geographic region or historical era. Many libraries will aggregate their reference materials on much the same system as the books in the stacks; knowing the call-number range of most of the books in your bibliography, you can shelf browse the same section in the reference room. Once you understand the layout, you will quickly discover a number of important and often fascinating reference tools. As you do, be sure to jot down the title and call number of each (or its location in the reference room) on a card. And don't hesitate to ask a reference librarian for help – both in finding relevant reference works and in using them.

Reference works can of course be located through the keyword or subject headings of the library catalog. But shelf browsing is apt to be particularly effective, especially if the materials in the reference room have the same call-number ranges as the books in the stacks on the same topics. If, for example, your topic is some aspect of the Spanish Civil War, you will notice that many of the call numbers of the books you have found start with DP (assuming that your library uses the Library of Congress classification system). DP is the classification for Spanish history. If you go to the DPs in the reference room, you will possibly discover a highly useful *Historical Dictionary of the Spanish Civil War,*

---

[6]　See for example Ronald H. Fritze, Brian E. Coutts, and Louis A. Vyhnanek (eds.), *Reference Sources in History: An Introductory Guide*, 2nd ed. (Santa Barbara, CA: ABC-CLIO, 2004).

1936–1939.[7] This volume provides a wealth of information on the major and minor figures of that conflict, plus descriptions of major parties, campaigns, and battles. There is a similar reference work on the Vietnam War, with entries for all the battles, campaigns, and major persons involved, plus a detailed chronology of events.[8] Those working in ancient history will find the nearly 1,200 pages of entries in *The New Century Classical Handbook* invaluable.[9]

The reference room also houses indexes to book reviews, such as the *Book Review Index* and the *Index to Book Reviews in Historical Periodicals*, both of which are likely to prove serviceable. The best way to find out what your library's reference room offers is simply to take some time to go on an exploratory journey around it.

The reference materials cited above are only a tiny sample of the riches that lie waiting in the reference room and elsewhere in your library. Whatever kind of paper you are writing and whatever its topic, there are bound to be reference materials of vital importance to you. Used intelligently in harness with your primary and secondary sources, they will both deepen your understanding and lighten your labors. Keep the holdings of the reference room in mind as we take up the writing of a historiographic essay and of a research paper in Chapters 6 and 7 respectively. But before considering how to write an account based on the sources you have located, let us consider, in the next chapter, how to get the most out of every source in your bibliography.

---

[7]   Edited by James W. Cortada (London: Greenwood Press, 1982). This is an example of a "split footnote," one in which part of the information regarding a publication – in this case the title – is given in the text, while the remaining data are in the footnote.

[8]   John S. Bowman, ed., *The Vietnam War: An Almanac,* with an introduction by Fox Butterfield (New York: World Almanac Publications, 1985).

[9]   Edited by Catherine B. Avery (New York: Appleton-Century-Crofts, 1962).

4

Getting the Most Out of History Books
Critical Reading and Assessment

The Need for More Effective Reading

In 1940 the eminent American scholar Mortimer Adler published a slim volume called *How to Read a Book*.[1] While the title might not seem the stuff of which bestsellers are made, Adler's work quickly rose to the top of the charts. Many readers were both curious and perplexed by the title. In a society that had only recently approached a condition of mass literacy, the great challenge, that of teaching the mechanics of reading, had been met. Reading a book, it was assumed, involved nothing more than a straightforward application of the ideas or skills it imparted. In short, reading a book was unproblematic. Yet one of the most respected educators in the United States obviously believed that effective, critically aware reading required an approach that went far beyond the application of basic rules. The enduring popularity

---

[1] Mortimer J. Adler, *How to Read a Book* (New York: Simon & Schuster, 1940). The latest English-language revision is Mortimer J. Adler and Charles Van Doren, *How to Read a Book* (New York: Simon & Schuster, 1972).

Going to the Sources: A Guide to Historical Research and Writing, Fifth Edition. Anthony Brundage.
© 2013 John Wiley & Sons, Ltd. Published 2013 by John Wiley & Sons, Ltd.

of *How to Read a Book* over the decades is testament to the validity of Adler's assertions. As history majors you are quickly made aware of what a reading-intensive discipline you have chosen. You are expected to read a great many books, essays, and articles, not only extracting factual information, but following interpretive arguments and placing the works in a historiographic context. In this chapter we will examine the challenges you face in attempting to understand historical scholarly works and to subject them to critical scrutiny. In doing so we will consider some of Adler's insights.

A commonsense view about the purpose of reading nonfiction works, especially those assigned in college courses, is that it consists in the extraction of information. With this goal in mind, conscientious readers jump into the book on page one and plow on through as expeditiously as possible, taking notes or, unless it is a library book, underlining and writing marginal comments. While this procedure usually proves effective for the extraction of some useful "facts," its efficacy will be greatly enhanced if it is preceded by some advance reconnaissance. The essential thing is to get a firm grasp of what the book is about and of where the author plans to take you. If that is not your starting point, you are dependent on each turn of the page to try to determine the author's overarching approach, purpose, and interpretation. It is like setting off on a cross-country car trip without a road map – or, for those with an inclination for such devices, without a GPS (global positioning satellite navigation system). In fact it is like driving off without having even glanced at a map beforehand. Applying this necessary preparation to the act of reading requires what Adler describes as "x-raying" a book,[2] by which he means discerning its skeletal structure at the outset. Once this information is gained, you can much more effectively navigate your way through the work at hand, significantly increasing both your understanding and your enjoyment.

The process of "x-raying" is not time-consuming, and it begins with a careful consideration of the title and subtitle of the book.

---

[2]   Adler and Van Doren, *How to Read a Book*, 75–95.

Authors choose their titles with care and try to convey to readers, as much as possible, the precise limits of the topic. This includes such matters as delimitations by place, time period, and type of history (political, military, social, economic, and so on). Often the most precise and valuable information about the scope of the book is found in the subtitle. A short amount of time spent pondering, through this deliberate consideration of the title, what type of book you are about to enter should be followed by a close inspection of the table of contents. Chapter titles, as well as the headings into which chapters are sometimes divided, are signposts that allow you to grasp in greater detail what you are about to encounter. They indicate the sequence of topics and provide a glimpse of the historical narrative to follow. Now you have at least consulted a map before driving off, and you have a rough idea of where the road will take you. It is now time to acquire some acquaintance with the author; but let us consider first why this might be of importance to the critical reader.

Finding out about Authors

Biographical details about the author, at least basic ones, are usually provided somewhere in the book. It is conventional to include a short paragraph about the writer on the dust jacket of a clothbound book or on the back cover of a paperback. In the case of a library book, the dust jacket is usually removed during cataloguing, though librarians sometimes clip and paste the biographical information inside the back cover. On the title page, an academic or other affiliation is often listed beneath the author's name. Just a few minutes spent in this manner can yield such basic items as the author's year of birth (sometimes listed on the copyright page), birthplace, professional affiliation, other publications, and possibly military service. The preface might yield important insights into why the author chose to write that particular book and into the perspective from which it has been written. The acknowledgments page and the dedication page might also prove helpful. In short, critical readers need to pay attention to the often neglected "front matter" of the book with which they are about to grapple. More extensive information than this requires going further afield, starting with an online search.

Many students might begin by typing the author's name into a major search engine such as Google, a procedure that has become so commonplace in recent years that virtually everyone in the online community knows the meaning of "googling." With luck, some very useful source like the author's resumé or *CV* (*curriculum vitae*, a Latin phrase meaning "life trajectory," under which one's professional life is summarized) might turn up near the top of the results. Usually, however, most of the hits will be things like listings of the author's various books on commercial sites like Amazon.com or the syllabi of instructors who assign particular books by that author for their courses. If a list of the author's books is all that such a search yields, you would be better served by just starting out with an Amazon.com search or with *Books in Print*, either in print or online. Since it will take only a few minutes to search websites such as Google or Amazon.com, starting there is a good idea. Be prepared, however, for results of limited usefulness. Even if you do have some luck with this kind of cursory research, you also need to consult more specialized online databases and printed collections available in or through your campus library. The *Biography and Genealogy Master Index* (*BGMI*) is the best single source to consult, as it will lead you to other online and printed sources such as *Who's Who in America*, the *Dictionary of Literary Biography*, or *Contemporary Authors*. Of course, it is possible, even with this more professional mode of research, that you come up empty-handed, especially if the author about whom you seek information is at the start of his or her career. Once you have done what you can on this matter, it is time to turn your attention to other parts of the book's front matter.

In your quest to determine the scope and orientation of the book prior to reading it, you have already carefully pondered its title and subtitle as well as the table of contents, and you have found out as much as you could about the author. Next, spend a few minutes reading the preface, the introduction, perhaps even the dedication page, to gain additional insights into why the author decided to write this particular book in this particular way. True, a dedication page is usually little more than a mention of a spouse, mentor, or other significant person in the author's life, but I once saw a dedication to a writer's parents, "farmers both."[3] Of what earthly use is this information, and why did the author want readers to know it? One needs to consider the book in question, which is a biographical study of William Cobbett, a journalist and political activist who devoted his life to championing the cause of agricultural laborers and small farmers in early nineteenth-century Britain. The author makes a persuasive case that this lowest social stratum of the English countryside was considerably more intelligent and perceptive about its real interests than is generally thought. That the author obviously considers his farm upbringing significant in the development of his interest in this topic is a reasonable surmise, though it is perhaps not of great importance. The point is that, by looking carefully at typically neglected portions of a book and by sensitizing ourselves to finding snippets of information that enlarge our understanding of the author's background, motives, and purposes, we are better prepared to engage in critical reading.

Comparing Similar Works of History

Perhaps the most effective way to grasp the process of active, critical reading is to compare two works that are, ostensibly, almost identical. The American Civil War is one of the most written about episodes in history. Thousands upon thousands of books, articles, and essays have considered the conflict from many different angles. Some authors have focused on the background of the war, others on its military, political, social, cultural, or economic dimensions, others still on its consequences. Some

---

[3] Ian Dyck, *William Cobbett and Rural Popular Culture* (Cambridge: Cambridge University Press, 1992), vii.

studies are general in nature, while others zero in on one individual or on a single battle or campaign. Some consider only a single state, district, or city. We will consider two significant histories of Washington, DC, during the Civil War – one published in 1941, the other in 2004. The classic study is Margaret Leech's *Reveille in Washington 1860–1865*; the recent work is Ernest B. Furgurson's *Freedom Rising: Washington in the Civil War*.[4] Since the books appear at first glance to be on the same subject, some readers might consider reading more than one of them superfluous. They could not be more wrong. There are major differences in approach, emphasis, and interpretation between the two works. Reading both of them would not only enrich your understanding of the life of the capital during the greatest crisis of the nation's history; it would also serve to show how very differently authors can frame a subject, narrate events, and judge facts and people.

Let us begin with the titles of the two works. Leech chose to call her book *Reveille in Washington*. Why? Consider the meaning of the word *reveille*. If this is a new term to you, the obvious course of action is to consult a dictionary. The English word "reveille" (pronounced rev-uh-lee) derives from the French noun *réveil* ("awakening"), which is in turn related to the verb *réveiller* ("to awaken"). Specifically, it is the name given to the lively martial music, often played on a bugle, used to rouse soldiers for the day's training or combat. So the title alone gives a clue to the fact that the author has framed her history around the idea or image of a city (and, by extension, a nation) that was metaphorically asleep in 1860. The raw, half-finished capital city, situated as it was on the very borders of the Confederacy, was surrounded by largely hostile populations in Maryland and Virginia. Indeed many Washingtonians favored the Confederacy, and the city was thick with spies. Militarily Washington was threatened from the outset with capture by enemy forces.

---

[4]   Margaret Leech, *Reveille in Washington 1860–1865* (New York: Harper & Brothers, 1941); Ernest B. Furgurson, *Freedom Rising: Washington in the Civil War* (New York: Alfred A. Knopf, 2004).

The Union's unpreparedness is underscored masterfully in Leech's first chapter, titled "The general is older than the capital." The chapter centers on the aging, corpulent Winfield Scott (1786–1866), general-in-chief of Union forces. Scott served under every president from Jefferson to Lincoln, masterminding the invasion of Mexico in 1847 along the way and being soundly defeated as the Whig party candidate for president in 1852. Vain, pompous, scarcely able to ride his horse even for short distances, and traumatized by the approaching conflagration, Scott is depicted as symptomatic of the Union army's many shortcomings in 1860. Its existing resources, both human and material, were woefully inadequate. Thus framed, Leech's account spoke directly to her readers in 1941, a time when World War II had been raging for two years and the likelihood of the United States' involvement was growing daily. To meet this near certainty, America on the eve of Pearl Harbor had one of the smallest armies of all the developed nations in the world. The rest of Leech's book hews to the military theme, though she by no means ignores the political and social history of the era.

Furgurson's book, *Freedom Rising*, written more than 60 years later, has a quite different emphasis, which is reflected in the title. A moment's reflection suggests that the freedom said to be rising must be that of African American slaves. This is indeed the case. Accordingly, Furgurson's first chapter is about the rancorous 1860 presidential election, with its vilifying by the slaveholding interests of even the most tepid abolitionists – and of Abraham Lincoln in particular – followed by eleven states' secession from the Union. A closer look, however, reveals that there is another meaning of *freedom* in the book; this is to be found in a short section that precedes the first chapter, which Furgurson calls a "prologue" (if you had decided to start your reading at the beginning of chapter 1 you would have missed it). The focus of the prologue is the nearly 20-foot high *Statue of Freedom* designed by the sculptor Thomas Crawford to top the still unfinished Capitol dome, the architect of which was Thomas Walter. A contentious work, Crawford's *Freedom* had originally worn a liberty cap, but in the hotly disputed run-up to the 1860 election this was changed to a helmet after a protest by Southern leaders, who were fearful that the liberty cap might serve as a potent symbol for those seeking to abolish slavery. This metaphor of the statue's meaning is pursued throughout the book, which concludes with a victory parade by masses of Union troops marshaling through Washington at the end of the war. The final sentence of the book is: "And soaring beyond the unending lines of blue, gleaming in the clear distance, Thomas Walter's dome atop the Capitol stood as it still stands, forever upholding the promise of Freedom."[5]

This inspiring ending, which ties in with the theme of the potent symbolism of the uncompleted *Statue of Freedom* developed by Furgurson in his preface, seems to come close to the conclusion of Leech's book:

> Across the Potomac, the guns had fallen silent. The guards were gone from the Washington bridges. Virginians were no longer enemies, but farmers who trundled their crops to the city markets. Rich with the wastage of armies, the perennial fields were green. On the Capitol dome, Armed Freedom rested on her sheathed sword.[6]

Yet, while there is a clear similarity, it is misleading. Note that Leech refers to the statue as "Armed Freedom" rather than just *Freedom* – though *Freedom* is what the sculpture has usually been called since its creation. She uses the same phrase in other references to the statue in her book. It is true that the statue's hand does rest lightly on the handle of a sword, though in the other she holds an olive branch, the symbol of peace. Leech's nomenclature clearly relates to her central theme, which is the Union's dramatic need for rapid rearmament and its development into a modern military power. Thus, even though both authors use the same symbol at the end of their books, the symbol stands for different things in their eyes. For Leech, the statue represents military victory, while for Furgurson it means emancipation.

---

[5]   Furgurson, *Freedom Rising*, 397.
[6]   Leech, *Reveille in Washington*, 419.

This difference in the authors' approaches is evident in the body of the two books. Of course, they both cover many of the same topics and the cast of characters is similar – from President Lincoln downward though to cabinet officials, military commanders, and hundreds of others. The same major events – including various battles, the issuance of the Emancipation Proclamation, and Lincoln's assassination – are covered in detail in both works. It is instructive, however, to compare the amount and sometimes the type of treatment given to each of these topics. The Emancipation Proclamation, for example, is given twice as much space by Furgurson, who also gives significant coverage to the leading black abolitionist Frederick Douglass, while Leech is contented with one brief mention of him. Leech also chose not to mention Sojourner Truth, the stalwart African American abolitionist, while Furgurson devotes five pages to her. Likewise, the crusading journalist and abolitionist Jane Grey Swisshelm receives extensive coverage in Furgurson's book, but is absent from Leech's. The same is true of the alluring Confederate spy Antonia Ford. While both authors write about Elizabeth Keckley, the black seamstress and confidante of Mary Todd Lincoln, Furgurson gives her substantially more treatment. Leech, on the other hand, lavishes attention on Union generals: between them, George B. McClellan and Irvin McDowell receive nearly twice the space given them by Furgurson.

There is more at work in these differences than merely one author's emphasis on generals over another's on abolitionists. We have to take into consideration the enormous changes in the historical profession that occurred between 1941 and 2004. To begin with, the state of Civil War historiography was very different in the earlier period. In the first decades of the twentieth century, a consensus had developed within the scholarly community that downplayed the role of slavery as a causative factor in the war. Constitutional principles such as "states' rights" and "national sovereignty" were said to be the underlying issues that triggered the conflict. There was a frankly patronizing tone on the part of many historians toward African Americans, who were treated largely as an inert force in Civil War history. In the late

1930s, when Leech was writing her book, scarcely any scholarly monographs on black history existed, and relatively few primary sources about blacks were available. Furgurson, on the other hand, was able to draw upon an enormous reserve of such primary and secondary sources.

In short, a revolution in the historiography of minorities in American life had taken place between the writing of the two works. The 1930s was also an era in which women's history had yet to emerge as a respected subfield of the discipline, and there were very few biographies and gendered histories of the Civil War for Leech to draw upon. These factors lie at the heart of the relative neglect of both blacks and women in Leech's book, by contrast to Furgurson's. There is also a substantial difference between the primary sources used by the authors, as even a quick glance at their bibliographies reveals. Leech conducted research on only four unpublished manuscript collections, while Furgurson consulted dozens (many of which were not available in Leech's day). Also, Furgurson was able to draw upon an invaluable online resource, the 128 volumes of the War Department's *Official Records of the Civil War*. The point is that Leech's relative neglect (and the word *relative* needs to be stressed) of blacks and women does not indicate that she was a racist or an antifeminist. It is clear from her account that she deplored slavery and had considerable sympathy with the women she did choose to portray. But books are, inescapably, products of the time and place in which they are written. This does not mean we should ignore older works and concentrate only on those written recently. As we have seen, there are emphases in Leech's account that are highly interesting and important. When we add her insights to Furgurson's, we have a much fuller grasp of the many dimensions of the topic. Reading both older and newer works on the same subject, when it is approached in the manner outlined in this chapter, also reveals how historiography evolves over time. The insights gained in such critical reading are essential in constructing a historiographic essay, which will be the centerpiece of Chapter 6.

Before taking up that project, let's consider two more pieces of unfinished business in the comparison between our two books on Washington during the Civil War: evaluating the quality of the writing; and finding information about the authors. When it comes to evaluating writing style, we are in the realm of a more subjective kind of appraisal than when we formally analyze the content of a book; yet style is surely one of the most important features of any work. The quality of a historian's prose not only determines whether or not a reader will persevere to the end, but also directly affects the accessibility of the information and the interpretation the author seeks to convey. Good writing is never just a "frill." Whether you consider history a social science or a branch of literature, the power to move, inspire, and, yes, even entertain your readers through the skillful deployment of words is vital. We often speak of a historian's ability to create "atmosphere," a sense that we are experiencing directly the historical settings and characters being depicted. This is an area in which no advantage of any kind can be ceded to modern authors. Avid readers have quickly recognized and responded to good writing since the time of Herodotus. It is above all the quality of writing that makes any history book a classic.

With this in mind, it must be said that, in the case of both books we have been comparing, the writing is superb. Any number of examples could be taken from either of them, but let's consider this passage from the opening chapter of *Freedom Rising* for its effectiveness in creating a sense of time and place:

> Politicians moving between White House and Congress, crinolined ladies moving from receptions to balls and recitals, ne'er-do-wells offering shady deals to visitors, all had to traverse streets deep with mud and muck in winter and clouded by dust in summer. Washington's unfinished Capitol stood above an unfinished city; less than seventy years before, the place had been woods, swamps and tobacco fields. Its few monumental government buildings and broad avenues were far out of scale with its scattered brick townhouses, rows of low-rise hotels and squalid slums of blacks and immigrants. Cattle, pigs and geese roamed free over broad empty

> stretches, including the acreage around the square stub of the
> Washington Monument, where indecision, vandalism and politics
> had halted construction at the 156-foot level.[7]

Note that this passage does not form part of the main narrative; it is provided in order to help the reader grasp the nature of the historical environment. Visual images are created in the mind, not only enhancing a reader's pleasure but establishing a physical setting in which the action of individuals and groups is played out. It is certainly true that such atmospherics can be overdone, resulting in a "picturesque" history that sacrifices some of the narrative momentum and perhaps a good deal of the analysis that readers expect. Used in due proportion, however, it brings a vital enhancement and rightly figures as one criterion for evaluating the worth of a book.

Finally, we need to consider biographical information about the authors, something that might indeed have topped the list of research items. A search through Google and through such databases as the *Dictionary of Literary Biography* serves us well, revealing both authors had a background in journalism. One interesting fact about Margaret Leech (1893–1974) that might help to explain her avid interest in American military preparedness on the eve of World War II is that, during World War I and well before the United States entered the conflict in 1917, she served as a volunteer in agencies assisting the Allied war effort. She was married to publisher Ralph Pulitzer – a connection that may raise the eyebrows of many a reader when they learn that *Reveille in Washington* won the Pulitzer Prize in history in 1942. However, as her obituary in the *New York Times* informs us, the Pulitzer family has no say in the awarding of the prize, this being entirely at the discretion of an independent jury appointed by Columbia University.[8] Leech received a second Pulitzer prize in 1960 for *In the Days of McKinley*.

As for Furgurson (born in 1929), the database *Contemporary Authors* gives us the outline of his professional life, including his

---

[7]   Furgurson, *Freedom Rising*, 13.
[8]   *New York Times*, February 25, 1974, p. 30.

service as a Marine Corps officer and a lengthy journalistic career with the *Baltimore Sun* (he was White House correspondent, Moscow Bureau Chief, and Saigon Bureau Chief during the Vietnam War). It also lists his other books, including two biographies (on General William C. Westmoreland and Senator Jesse Helms), two histories of Civil War battles (Chancellorsville and Cold Harbor), and a study of the Confederate capital, Richmond, during the war. Thus it is clear that Furgurson had already established himself as a military historian of note and had foreshadowed his study of wartime Washington with an earlier book on Richmond. His many works reveal a fascination not only with the Civil War, but also with Southern life and culture (both Westmoreland and Helms were Southerners), and it comes as no surprise to learn that Furgurson grew up in Virginia – a fact he discloses in the preface to *Freedom Rising*, together with a brief mention that his great-grandparents were proud Confederates.[9] A Google search of the author leads us to his publisher's website, and there we find an interview in which Furguson expands on the role of his Virginia upbringing in prompting him to write about the Civil War:

> When I was a child, the Civil War seemed all around me. All of my great-grandfathers had been Confederate soldiers. I grew up in Danville, Virginia, the last capital of the Confederacy; I went to Robert E. Lee grammar school and played the part of Lee in our fifth-grade pageant in Virginia.[10]

Nothing illustrates better how motives of a deeply personal nature often impel a person to spend years researching and writing particular books in particular ways; and this is why it is important for you to learn as much as you can about an author before evaluating his or her book.

---

[9] Furgurson, *Freedom Rising*, xi.
[10] At http://www.randomhouse.com/knopf/catalog/display.pperl?isbn=9780 375404542&view=qa (accessed November 21, 2006).

Reviewing a History Book

Whether you are going to write a book report or something lengthier and more complex, such as a historiographic essay, the process discussed above will help you get a handle on any book and see what makes it distinctive. Even if the assignment you are completing does not require you to make a formal comparison with books on the same topic, it can prove helpful to get hold of at least one more book on that topic and engage in a little "x-raying." To recapitulate, the elements of an effective review can be summarized as follows:

- biographical information gleaned from printed and online sources about the author and what certain elements in the author's career might suggest about why and how that author wrote on that subject;
- what the author has to say about such matters in sections of the book such as the preface, dedication, and acknowledgments;
- the methodological emphasis of the book, including whether it is primarily a book of political, social, economic, or some other kind of history;
- the structure of the book as is revealed in the title, subtitle, and chapter headings;
- the nature of the sources employed by the author, including how much unpublished manuscript material was consulted;
- the author's overarching interpretation and the degree to which this can be said to be revisionist. Sometimes the author will be very explicit about his interpretation, while in other cases it will be necessary to compare it to others in similar books;
- the quality of the writing;
- any obvious signs of bias or partisanship.

These points need to be borne in mind when researching and writing a historiographic essay, in which a number of books, articles, and essays on a given topic are compared and woven into a comprehensive treatment. As you undertake such an assignment, keep in mind that the same methods for determining the nature of a history book work equally well when you are dealing with an article or other shorter form of writing. Before turning our attention to the writing of a historiographic essay or of a longer history thesis, let us examine in the next chapter the use of nontextual sources by historians.

5

Beyond Textual Sources
Historians' Use of Other Media

Words, Images, and the Historical Imagination

Whenever we ponder past events, it is not only a set of historical facts that comes to mind, but a rich array of images. Not only are these images an inseparable and necessary component of historical knowledge, but they are hard-wired into the way we think. The histories we fashion, whether presented orally or in writing, conjure up pictures in the minds of our listeners or readers. Of course, the same holds true for novels and poems, but also for works of science and technology. Given the centrality of images in human understanding, it is not surprising that writers in all fields have often tried over the ages to supplement words with pictures. Indeed, considering that the largest part of humankind, in all societies, has been illiterate until recent times, images (including three-dimensional ones, like statues and temples) have been vastly more important than the written word in conveying the essence of political, social, and religious institutions and beliefs, as well as society's past. But, since it is the literate

Going to the Sources: A Guide to Historical Research and Writing, Fifth Edition.
Anthony Brundage.
© 2013 John Wiley & Sons, Ltd. Published 2013 by John Wiley & Sons, Ltd.

present that we operate in, we will keep our focus on the interplay between text and image.

In modern times, the most obvious way in which specific images are given to readers is through the use of photos – a practice so widespread and of such obvious value that there is little need to dwell on it. However, one might still ask whether such illustrations serve an essential purpose, or whether they simply enhance the sense of immediacy, of "being there," in the historical moment. A book on the dropping of atomic bombs on Japan is rendered much more powerful and immediate through the inclusion of photographs of the massive destructions at Hiroshima and Nagasaki. This is one reason for the persistence of the tired cliché "a picture is worth a thousand words." While this holds true in certain cases, it is also true that a few dozen well-chosen words can impart much more than a thousand pictures can, for words alone can convey mental states (say, that of President Truman when he ordered the nuclear attacks, or that of dazed survivors trying to comprehend the horror through which they were living). Words, not images, are necessary to discuss policy, strategy, or any other form of intentionality. And words are our only path to an understanding of the functioning of past societies, of the central beliefs and values of their peoples, and of the countless elements of past lives that no picture can provide or for which no image is available. To put it another way, for historians, words are essential while images are supplemental.

That said, we must consider another, much more powerful visual technology, albeit one that grew out of photography: motion pictures. Unlike photographs, films do not serve as direct illustrative material for textual accounts. Rather they operate independently and in a kind of rivalry with the printed word. And when it comes to conveying a sense of history to the majority of the world's population, for the past century and longer motion pictures have been far more important than books. In the last half century television has played a similar role. Because of the power and pervasiveness of these "moving-pictures" media, we need to consider the relationship between the kind of historical knowledge they convey and that provided by books. We begin by a consideration of one of the most popular and powerful of all the motion pictures of the early twentieth century.

The Birth of a Nation: Entertainment, Propaganda, and Critical Response

Just after the turn of the twentieth century, Thomas Dixon (1864–1946), who had tried his hand successfully as a preacher, actor, lawyer, and legislator, published a series of melodramatic novels about the Civil War and Reconstruction. These volumes, *The Leopard's Spots* (1902), *The Clansman* (1905), and *The Traitor* (1907), were to be the foundation of perhaps the most effective and controversial motion picture ever made for mass consumption in the United States. Born in North Carolina during the final year of the Civil War, Dixon grew up during a bitter and turbulent era, one marked by Southerners' deep resentment toward the Confederacy's loss of the war and toward Northerners' attempts to reconstruct Southern society and to advance the interests of the newly freed slaves or "freed people." Dixon's books were bestsellers, and they particularly appealed to D. W. Griffith (1875–1948), a major film director of the period who was on the lookout for material to be turned into an epic film the likes of which no one had yet produced. Griffith, whose father had served as a colonel in the Confederate army, was sympathetic to Dixon's pro-Southern message, and the two became close collaborators. Until that time, even the longest silent films were no longer than one hour; many were 15-minute one-reelers, cranked out quickly on low budgets. *The Birth of a Nation*, when it was released in early 1915, cost a staggering $112,000 and had a running time of three hours and ten minutes.

The story, based mainly on *The Clansman* but incorporating elements from the other novels, begins just before the Civil War. Ranting abolitionists are shown denouncing slavcowners as vicious and inhuman. This is followed by an idyllic view of the Cameron plantation in South Carolina, with its benevolent master and its well-cared for, contented slaves. Young brothers of the Stoneman family from Pennsylvania pay a visit to their close friend Ben, son and heir of the Cameron family. Thus the film establishes at the outset a close bond between a Northern and a Southern family, one that will become even closer as the daughters of each family are drawn into romantic matches with the sons of the other. Movie viewers watched in fascinated horror as these relationships were rent asunder by the madness, hatred, and destruction of the Civil War. Both families lose sons and, in one especially melodramatic scene, a Stoneman and a Cameron are killed in the same battle, their corpses lying near each other. For the survivors, friendship and romance must be placed on hold until the end of hostilities and the misguided, destructive early years of Reconstruction. Indeed the post-Civil War era takes up more than two thirds of the film, and it is clear that the alleged evils of Reconstruction were the main target of Dixon and Griffith.

We might expect that such a pro-Confederacy film would give a highly negative portrayal of Abraham Lincoln, whose election in 1860 was the trigger for the secession of Southern states. On the contrary, the president is depicted as deeply aggrieved at the massive destruction and loss of life, and eager to bind up the wounds of war without rancor or revenge. While radical Republican leaders in Congress push for a vindictive treatment of the conquered Confederate states, Lincoln shows compassion, at one point saying: "I shall deal with them as if they had never been away." His assassination shortly after the war ruins any chance of a wise and temperate policy. Unleashed by radical Republican leaders (including Congressman Austin Stoneman, head of the Stoneman family and a character closely modeled on Thaddeus Stevens), black federal troops and carpetbaggers are shown taking charge of the district of South Carolina, where the old Cameron plantation is located. Vivid images are shown of whites being treated contemptuously by black troops no less than by recently freed slaves.

The most viciously racist portrayals begin at this point in the film. With the exception of a few loyal servants who remain with their masters, African Americans are depicted as either child-like simpletons, easily manipulated by others, or as vicious, lustful animals, eager to prey on white womanhood. In case any viewers missed the point, Griffith offered an explanation on the screen by quoting a passage from one of the leading textbooks of American history (for the source, see below):

> Adventurers swarmed out of the North, as much the enemies of one race as of the other, to cozen, beguile, and use the negroes. [...] In the villages were the office-holders, men who knew none of the uses of authority, except its insolences. [...] The policy of the congressional leaders wrought [...] a veritable overthrow of civilization in the South [...] in their determination to put the white South under the heel of the black South.

In the remaining hour or so of the film, Griffith introduces more and more scenes of uncivilized blacks abusing power and attacking or lusting after white women. When Congressman Stoneman arrives in the area for an inspection, he is accompanied by his daughter Elsie, played by the lovely queen of silent-era cinema, Lillian Gish (1893–1993). Elsie has formed an attachment to Ben Cameron but finds herself courted ardently by a powerful black man, elected to the post of lieutenant-governor in a rigged election. Thus it is not just white Southern women who are threatened by blacks, but Northern women too. Northerners like Elsie, as well as her father, are made to realize the grievous error they made in assuming that blacks could be safely promoted to a position of equality with whites. Such policies could only lead to miscegenation – the sexual mingling of whites and blacks, which was widely regarded in that era as an abomination and was to be made illegal in a majority of states.

It is pointless to pursue the twists and turns of the melodramatic plot any further. Instead our focus should be on the larger historical interpretation the story offers. Griffith was clearly steering audiences to the view that a great crisis had been reached in post-Civil War Southern society, one brought on not only by military defeat, but especially by the vindictive policies of a Congress dominated by radical Republicans. At stake was the very survival of American civilization, which was inseparably bound up with white supremacy. In the film, the solution to this dire turn of events is the spirited uprising of the aggrieved Southern whites, who form themselves into the Ku Klux Klan and heroically battle the upstart African Americans, successfully restoring the "natural" social and racial order. And, to drive home his point about the necessary reconciliation of white Northerners and Southerners, Griffith shows a group of Union army veterans fighting side by side with the Klansmen against blacks, while this caption appears on the screen: "Former enemies united by their Aryan blood."

Before examining what audiences took away from this epic film as well as the broader public reaction to it, we need to consider the key role played by yet another Southerner: President Woodrow Wilson (1856–1924). Born in Virginia just before the Civil War, Wilson, like Dixon and Griffith, grew up in an atmosphere of deep resentment toward the Confederate loss and toward what was viewed in the South as the vindictive policies of Congress during Reconstruction. Wilson became friends with Dixon when they were both in the PhD program in history at Johns Hopkins University in Maryland. Dixon left Hopkins after a short time, while Wilson completed his doctorate and went on to become president of Princeton University and governor of New Jersey before being elected President of the United States in 1912. He was the first holder of a PhD to fill the presidency, and also the first to show a feature-length motion picture in the White House. The film, of course, was *The Birth of a Nation*, which Wilson reportedly described as "history written in lightning."

Not only was Wilson a fan of the movie, but his words were quoted on the screen. The passage (reproduced above) that Griffith cited on screen from a leading US history textbook was in fact from Wilson's *History of the American People*.[1] Just how close Wilson's views were to those of Dixon and Griffith also can be gathered from in another passage from his book:

---

[1]   Woodrow Wilson, *A History of the American People* (New York: Harper & Brothers, 1906), vol. 5, 49.

The white men of the South were aroused by a mere instinct of self-preservation to rid themselves, by fair means or foul, of the intolerable burden of governments sustained by the votes of ignorant negroes and conducted in the interest of adventurers: governments whose incredible debts were incurred that thieves might be enriched, whose increasing loans and taxes went to no public use but into the pockets of party managers and corrupt contractors. There was no place of open action or of constitutional agitation, for the men who were the real leaders of the southern communities.[2]

And, as president, Wilson promoted the racial segregation of federal departments that had been integrated since Reconstruction. Thus we witness an extraordinary alliance between a novelist, a filmmaker, and the president of the United States in promulgating a view of history according to which the Civil War had been unnecessary, the Reconstruction policies inflicted on the South by a victorious Union were unjust and destructive, and members of the Ku Klux Klan, a brazenly racist and violent organization, were the heroic redeemers of civilization.

How did this cinematic interpretation of history compare with that offered by the new class of professional historians of the era? At one level, it must be said that the views expressed in the film were not that far removed from those of the academic specialists. The leading authority at the time was Professor William A. Dunning (1857–1922) of Columbia University, whose books on Reconstruction made some of the same points as the film regarding Northern policies in the defeated South. The views of Dunning and other like-minded historians (often referred to as "the Dunning school") were dominant in the first half of the twentieth century. Yet there were important differences from the interpretations offered in *The Birth of a Nation*. The academic views were considerably more complex and nuanced. While some degree of racial prejudice is discernible in the historians' accounts, they did engage in careful research on masses of primary sources and made a number of important breakthroughs in our understand-

---

[2]   Ibid., 58.

ing of the post-Civil War era. Perhaps most importantly, their work, while by no means free of some racial stereotyping, is not marked by the virulent racism and sexually charged paranoia of the motion picture. In short, the written histories did not stir people's passions. The amount of time it takes one to absorb, reflect on, and react to written accounts (in the form of offering alternative interpretations) can be considerable. In stark contrast, motion pictures are an inherently "hot" medium, which by its nature makes a direct emotional and visceral appeal on the viewer. Caught up in the film's momentum and swept along through often intense imagery, the viewer has little opportunity to consider the veracity of the film as history. We should also note that this "silent" picture had a musical score especially written for it that incorporates segments of well-known tunes like "Dixie," played in larger theaters by full orchestras, in smaller ones by a piano or organ player, all helping to create an even more intense emotional experience.

What then, did the audiences of the day carry away after viewing the film? Did they fall lock-step behind the contentions of Dixon and Griffith? It is of course impossible to answer that question. What can be said is that the film was an enormous hit, many people returning to see it many times over and applauding wildly at especially stirring moments. A lot of this was due to the high level of Griffith's directorial skill. He was a master film-maker, and he introduced a number of effective innovations like the tracking shot, night filming, and the use of red color filters on scenes of battle and other high-impact episodes. He had even considered shooting it in a primitive color process called Kine Color, though in the end he rejected it for financial and technical reasons. Another innovation was his insertion of several well-crafted "historical facsimiles" throughout the film – such as the assassination of Lincoln at Ford's Theater and the surrender of Confederate General Robert E. Lee to Union General Ulysses S. Grant at Appomattox – in which great efforts were made to achieve historical accuracy in every detail. The use of these detailed vignettes magnified the sense in viewers' minds that they were witnessing a recreation of history, as opposed to a film based on a novel. No doubt, for most of those who sat in the theater transfixed for three hours, it was primarily an exciting and enjoyable movie; but it is hard to escape the conclusion that many viewers emerged with an enhanced sense of white supremacy and of the wrongs done to the South by the federal government. While it is difficult to demonstrate it conclusively, this was almost certainly a factor in the revival, in the wake of the film, of the Ku Klux Klan in the 1920s and 1930s and in its spread to various places in Northern states.

Finally, we should note that the American public's reaction to *The Birth of a Nation* was by no means entirely positive. Many Americans took grave offense at Griffith's creation, and numerous protests against the showing of the film were staged in cities throughout the United States, many of them led by members of the recently founded National Association for the Advancement of Colored People (NAACP). In some of these demonstrations African Americans were joined by significant numbers of whites. Indeed the film helped call attention not only to the revival of the Ku Klux Klan, but to the Jim Crow laws and practices, which were still pervasive throughout the South, and to the ongoing atrocity of the lynching of African Americans at the hands of white vigilantes. For growing numbers of Americans, *The Birth of a Nation* became firmly linked to racism and oppression. That messages of hate could be encapsulated in films of high entertainment value helped make some people aware of the enormous power of film to spread both good will and evil. While it might be argued that this critical awareness of the potentials and pitfalls of the medium of film was not widespread, the growth of educational opportunities at least made it possible for more people to resist the superficial blandishments of a movie's allure. This became essential as the power of imagery was magnified with the technological advances made in the second half of the twentieth century.

D. W. Griffith was of course not the only American creating historically themed "epic" motion pictures in the silent-film era and into the sound era after 1928. There was, for example, Cecil B. DeMille (1881–1959), who directed a number of big productions over a nearly 40-year span, many of them lavish epics based on the Bible. Nor was epic filmmaking based on history confined to that of the United States. Some of the most inventive film-makers active in the first half of the twentieth century were Europeans like the French Director Abel Gance (1889–1981). Gance's masterpiece was the monumental *Napoléon* (1927), which kept audiences riveted in their seats for the nearly six hours of its running time (in the original version) and incorpo-rated experimental techniques such as hand-held cameras, the superimposing of images, and wide-screen sequences using three cameras. The propaganda power of such epic filmmaking was not lost on the rising dictatorships of the age. In particular, the Soviet Union under Josef Stalin and Nazi Germany under Adolf Hitler made highly effective use of motion pictures to bind the masses to their regimes. The Third Reich was powerfully bolstered by the films of Leni Riefenstahl (1902–2003), the first female film-maker to achieve international fame. Her *Triumph of the Will*, made at the 1934 rally of the Nazi Party at Nuremburg, set the standard for propaganda films, and to this day it can have a mes-merizing effect on an unwary viewer.

Technological and creative improvements in filmmaking con-tinued into the second half of the twentieth century, and there was a corresponding growth in the making of documentary films, many of which dealt with historical topics. Many of these works were made for the newer medium of television, which, with the growth of the cable industry, came to have channels dedicated entirely to studies of the past, such as the History Channel.[3] In the next section we will compare the treatment of the same event – namely the plot to kill Hitler – in a recent book, in a straight-forward documentary film, and in a feature-length Hollywood movie. Of course there are numerous books as well as film treat-ments of this subject, but a comparison of these three, all released in 2008, should prove instructive.

---

[3] In this channel's first few years of operation, programming was so overwhelm-ingly dedicated to World War II, and especially to the Third Reich, that critics dubbed it the "Hitler Channel."

Reading, Viewing, Reflecting: A Case Study

Adolf Hitler's seizure of supreme authority in interwar Germany occurred, like the rise of the Ku Klux Klan, in the turmoil of a defeated and embittered country suffering under foreign occupation. Jews became the scapegoats for the Nazi Party just as African Americans had been for the Klan. The German upheaval made it possible for an obscure Austrian with little or no prospect of worldly success to rise to the pinnacle of power. Many traditional conservative elements of society – especially in the Junker class, from which the bulk of German military leadership had always sprung – took a dim view of this ignorant upstart. However, given Hitler's hypnotic hold on large segments of the population, even the strongest of the military leaders were unable to challenge his absolute power during the first years of the Third Reich. Later, when his ever-more aggressive foreign policy and his launching of a new world war threatened to destroy the nation, some members of the Junker class were moved to act. The result was a complex array of plotters, most of them from the officer corps, some working at cross-purposes, but all with a common goal: the elimination of Hitler and the negotiation of peace with Germany's enemies. Before looking at the treatments offered by the book's author and by the filmmakers, it is important to note that, unlike Dixon and Griffith in regard to the Confederacy, none of them has, for a goal, the changing of previously negative views into positive ones. All clearly sympathize with the plotters and believe it would have been good if they had succeeded, thus removing a hugely destructive madman from the scene. All of them also agree on the basic components of the story, differing only (but significantly) on the factors they believe were most important to the plot. Thus the question is not, as it was with *The Birth of a Nation*, one of examining the peculiar power of film to persuade, but rather the strengths and weaknesses of each kind of treatment of the same topic.

On July 20, 1944, Hitler was discussing Eastern Front strategy with his generals at the Wolf's Lair, the Führer's heavily fortified and secure headquarters in East Prussia. A powerful bomb exploded during the meeting, killing several of those present but sparing Hitler. Amidst conflicting rumors in Berlin and elsewhere about whether the assassination attempt had succeeded, some army plotters began their move to seize power. They used an existing program named Operation Valkyrie, which had been designed to thwart military takeovers and to counter civil unrest, while others would back away. When it became clear that Hitler had indeed survived, retribution was quick and merciless. It was discovered that the head of the conspiracy, indeed the man who planted the bomb, was a dashing and charismatic colonel, Count Claus von Stauffenberg. His execution was immediate and was followed, during succeeding months, by that of 5,000 others. It seems a straightforward enough tale, but, when historians gained access to mountains of primary-source material after the German defeat, they discovered that the events of July 1944 were but the tip of an iceberg. There had been numerous plots before, all of them going awry, sometimes at the very last minute. Thus historians or filmmakers had to construct a complex story, setting forth the connections between these plots and plotters without overwhelming readers/viewers with confusing masses of details. Let us examine how each went about this task.

In a recent book titled *Countdown to Valkyrie*, British author Nigel Jones weaves an exciting tale, beginning with the events of July 20, 1944 and then backing up to provide explanations of how Stauffenberg and his fellow plotters took up and tried to succeed against heavy odds.[4] Considerable space is devoted to Stauffenberg, including his aristocratic childhood and education. The middle third of the book is given over to the rise of Hitler and the Nazis to power, the gathering of the storm clouds of war, and the early plots against the Führer. With the outbreak of World War II, Jones brings Stauffenberg back into the story, showing his bravery in battle (he lost a hand and an eye in North Africa), but also his growing moral revulsion at the German

---

[4] Nigel Jones, *Countdown to Valkyrie: The July Plot to Assassinate Hitler* (London: Frontline Books, 2008).

atrocities carried out under Hitler's orders. The other major conspirators, while not covered in equally great detail, are given
sufficient space to appear on stage as vivid individuals. This is an
area where the book shows its superiority to film. To have 40
characters play significant parts in a screen dramatization can
quickly overwhelm the viewer. While this can happen in a book
as well, Jones makes it easier for readers by including a glossary
of the individuals at the end of the book, each with a capsule
biography, so readers can easily check (and recheck) the facts on
someone they might have forgotten about. The author is also
especially generous in his interpretation of Stauffenberg's and the
others' motives: "They may have failed to kill Hitler, but in
the mere fact of making the attempt these brave men snatched the
soul of their tortured country from the pit – and saved it."[5]

A well-produced 76-minute television documentary, *Operation
Valkyrie: The Stauffenberg Plot to kill Hitler*, shows some of the
advantages offered by a film treatment of a topic. Like Jones's
book, it begins with the events of July 20, 1944 and moves back
to earlier phases in the life of Claus von Stauffenberg, as well as
to key earlier events in German history. Although the book is
amply illustrated with black-and-white photos, obviously the
documentary's use of motion pictures, including a fair amount
of archival footage, is more effective. In a relatively short film,
while the coverage of main highlights concerning the rise of
Nazism and Hitler's takeover is somewhat cursory, it must be said
that the background of the other major plotters is done very well.
The treatment of the nature of the bomb that Stauffenberg
brought in his briefcase to the Wolf's Lair on July 20 is explained
quite effectively, as are the construction of the bunker where the
meeting was supposed to be held and the map room where it
was moved because of the hot weather. By showing diagrams of
the room itself and of the huge oak conference table, both of
which were crucial to the effect of the bomb blast, and then by
rotating them as 3D models on the screen, the filmmaker achieves
a much higher level of vividness and clarity than is possible with

---

[5]   Ibid., xi.

the printed word. While Jones makes the same point about the fact that the move to the map room saved Hitler's life – because the windows allowed much of the blast's force to be dissipated outward and the oak table shielded him – the film demonstrates it much more effectively.

Finally, the high-budget, star-studded Hollywood version of the topic is given in *Valkyrie*. The film, directed by Bryan Singer and starring Tom Cruise and Kenneth Branagh, of course has higher production values than the documentary. This adds to the emotional impact, but in a sense it comes at a cost: our awareness that we are watching a movie, due to the presence of very well known movie stars like Cruise on the screen. Like the book and the documentary, the movie starts with an exciting event – not the bomb at the Wolf's Lair, but the attack on Stauffenberg's unit in North Africa by British planes, leaving him severely wounded and musing about the rightness of the war. The rest of the film goes over much the same material, but, it must be said, it does far less to cover the array of military men involved in the plot. By concentrating on about a half dozen of the conspirators, the movie omits some key figures. Unlike in the book and documentary, there is nothing here on General Erwin Rommel, one of the best known German military leaders, who was an active conspirator by 1944 but whose wounding in an Allied attack left him unable to participate. Apart from such omissions, the movie had some obviously excellent historical advisors (a minor career option for professional historians).

The Evolving Integration of Text and Image

As this rather cursory examination of the three treatments of the plot to kill Hitler suggests, there are strengths and weaknesses to each mode of presentation. While the visual media have a clear advantage in vividness and impart a sense of immediacy or of "being there," the book's superiority lies in enabling the reader to stop at will to reflect upon or critique what has just been read, as well as to check on forgotten persons or incidents by turning to the book's index or glossary. While it is true that one can also readily stop and rewind video recordings for the same purposes, the inherent momentum of the film-watching process makes it far less likely that a viewer would be prompted to take any such steps. Reading is uniquely well suited to an individual's critical response to what is being presented. The written word and the imagery are being increasingly interwoven with the help of modern technology, but it is safe – as well as gratifying – to predict that the history book in its standard format, illustrated by nothing more than photos and maps, is not going to disappear any time soon, even as e-books in their many forms are certain to play an increasing role. In the ongoing integration of printed and e-book material, the key will be to ensure that the critical functions associated with reading remain paramount in whichever form of media and on whatever type of device we experience history.

Finally, the categories of "historian" and "filmmaker" are no longer as discrete and different as they have been presented in this chapter. An increasing number of professional historians have made it their mission to produce documentary films, and some special graduate programs are available to train such individuals. The American Historical Association (AHA) now gives an annual prize, the John E. O'Connor Film Award, in recognition of outstanding interpretations of history through film or video. For all of us who have a deep interest in the past, the interaction between words and images has an exciting and creative future.

6

Exploring Changing Interpretations

The Historiographic Essay

In this chapter we will explore more fully the nature of the revisionist process by considering the writing of a historiographic essay. In Chapter 1 we examined a few of the major currents in historiography in the broadest sense of the word – that is, the history of historical writing. Now we will consider historiography in its narrower meaning – the variety of approaches, methods, and interpretations employed by historians on a particular topic. The historiographic essay is an important literary form in its own right, endowing the reader with a sense of how the topic in which he or she is interested has been approached by previous scholars. An awareness of the historiography of your topic is an essential prerequisite to undertaking research and writing that use primary sources. Knowing the kinds of approaches and interpretations already employed by others as well as the still unanswered questions on your topic can help direct your inquiry along original lines. The writing of a historiographic essay is also an excellent learning exercise, since in order to write one it is

Going to the Sources: A Guide to Historical Research and Writing, Fifth Edition.
Anthony Brundage.
© 2013 John Wiley & Sons, Ltd. Published 2013 by John Wiley & Sons, Ltd.

necessary to become immersed in the intellectual processes of historians as they modify and revise our views of the past.

Selecting and Refining a Topic

Selecting and refining a topic is vitally important. Many students are inclined to choose a particularly vivid historical incident like the Japanese attack on Pearl Harbor or the assassination of Abraham Lincoln, in the belief that it will prove both interesting and manageable. In this they are not deceived. The intrinsic human drama of such events, together with their being limited to short and specific spans of time, makes them attractive research topics for the busy undergraduate. This is no doubt a major reason why a topic in military history is often a first choice. Another is that in many cases the survey courses students have encountered emphasize military conflicts and the more dramatic political events. Indeed many of these are quite suitable subjects for a historiographic essay, since they have been approached and interpreted by historians in a variety of ways. But before seizing too readily on one of the more "famous" topics, it is worth your while to ponder the many alternatives open to you.

For example, there is a great abundance of fascinating subjects in social history, each with a rich and varied historiography. Numerous books, articles, and essays have been written on aspects of the history of education, sexuality, trade unions, sports, religion, immigration, popular entertainment, and crime. The history of science, technology, or industry also comprises viable and interesting topics. You may feel a bit uncomfortable selecting a less familiar topic, but doing so will offer you greater opportunities for expanding your intellectual horizons. Even if you choose a biographical topic, it need not concern a well-known political or military figure. Many thousands of fascinating people in all fields of endeavor throughout history have been the subject of significant scholarly attention.

The initial selection of a topic usually needs to be followed by a process of refining. Frequently the subject, as it is first conceptualized, turns out to be too broad; occasionally it is too narrow. You would soon discover, for example, that a topic like "Renaissance humanism" is extraordinarily vast and complex. It has such an extensive literature that you could not hope to find, read, and analyze more than a tiny fraction of it within the time constraints of your course and the space limitations of your paper. Even a reduction in the scope of the topic, say, to "Renaissance humanism in Florence" would still be too broad, though such a geographic narrowing of the subject is moving you toward something manageable. In addition to giving your paper this geographic focus, you could also limit its scope topically, chronologically, or biographically. A combination of these methods of narrowing is exemplified in a research paper title like "The Medici and civic humanism in fifteenth-century Florence." Even this topic may require additional refinement, but clearly it is much more viable than the first choice – or even the second. Probably the precise scope of your paper will not be defined until you have gained a clearer notion of the dimensions of the topic's historiography.

Research for a Historiographic Essay: A Case Study

The finding of historical sources was described in general terms in the last chapter; now we will examine the process as it applies to a specific topic. The example we will consider is an essay of about 4,500 words written by Patricia J. Autran, a student in my History Methods class.[1] The assignment was to write a historiographic essay of approximately 20 pages based on 15 to 20 secondary sources. Her paper is titled "The Lewis and Clark Expedition: Changing interpretations." This essay serves well as an example, since it cuts across a number of important topics in American history: exploration, westward expansion, scientific inquiry, encounters with indigenous peoples, the role of women,

---

[1] I wish to express my gratitude to Ms. Autran for permission to reproduce her paper.

and attitudes towards the natural environment – to name a few. It obviously has important biographical dimensions, too; not only through Meriwether Lewis and William Clark, but through such figures as Thomas Jefferson, who envisaged and launched the enterprise, and Sacagawea, the Native American woman who helped guide it.

In searching for books on this topic, the initial step is the logical one of doing a library catalog search by using the keywords "lewis and clark." Depending upon the extent of your library's holdings, this step alone should take you to dozens, perhaps even hundreds of titles. Having hit such a large number of titles can produce a sinking feeling. How can you be expected to winnow this down to a manageable number of titles, especially considering that these are just the books? You still have to search for articles and essays. Be of good cheer – the challenge is not as formidable as it appears. The key is to remain focused and systematic. The first thing to do is to keep in mind that you are looking for secondary works. Scrolling through the list of sources quickly shows that many of the titles are various editions of the journals of Lewis and Clark. They are primary sources – essential reading if you are undertaking a paper about the expedition itself; but remember, you are writing about historians and the different ways they have approached and interpreted the topic. Therefore you should consider only the secondary sources on the list. You can further exclude anything that is described on the catalog entry as "juvenile literature." The list is already considerably shorter, and not much time has been expended. What next?

Since the assignment is a historiographic essay, and therefore you want to explore as many different kinds of interpretation as possible, let that concern guide your further winnowing of sources. Titles and subtitles of books will usually give you a good idea of their scope and approach. Try to select works with as many approaches to the topic as possible. From the titles, it will be evident that some works are general in character, others have a biographical focus, while others deal with topics like the scientific observations of the expedition, relations with Native Americans, and so on. This provides a basis for further selection;

but at this point you need to go to the library stacks to have a look at the volumes you have identified for possible inclusion in your bibliography. Examining the books for apparent depth, scholarly rigor, and interpretive interest may take some time, and it involves looking at such matters as bibliographies, footnotes, and possibly even the author's academic credentials. This may not help you much in deciding between one scholarly book and another when drastic pruning is called for, but at least it should be possible to exclude works that are clearly superficial and unscholarly.

At this point you would be well advised to look at some recent scholarly books on the subject to see which secondary sources the authors of those books consider important. Perhaps in perusing the list of authors in your catalog search you recognized the name Stephen E. Ambrose, one of America's leading historians. Among his many books is *Undaunted Courage: Meriwether Lewis, Thomas Jefferson, and the Opening of the American West* (1996). Even if you had not heard of him before, a perusal of his volume in the stacks would make the value of his book evident. Examining the titles in the bibliography of his book, and perhaps also looking to see which sources he frequently cites in his endnotes, will assist you in further refining your selection of titles for your own bibliography. (In addition to this, you should also check out the Ambrose volume and begin reading it, because you need to acquire more factual knowledge of the topic in order to complete your search for titles.) One very likely result of perusing Ambrose's bibliography is that it will bring to your attention important sources that your own library does not have among its holdings. These can be ordered through interlibrary loan. You should also search any database of libraries affiliated with your own, to find titles that your library does not possess. WorldCat (described in Chapter 3) might also be helpful, though it is such a massive database that a simple search under "lewis and clark" is likely to produce thousands of hits. On the other hand, a "sacagawea" search in WorldCat is sure to produce a more manageable list of titles. When using WorldCat, always remember to use the search-reducing features described in Chapter 3.

In the search for scholarly articles on this topic, the online database (or the bound volume index) *America: History and Life* will prove especially valuable. The *Humanities Index* (either online, as part of WilsonWeb, or in bound-volume format) and the ArticleFirst database should also yield some good titles. Depending on the array of databases available in your library, other indexes and abstracts may also prove useful. These include some full-text databases such as JSTOR. By giving you immediate access to the complete article online, full-text databases will save time, especially if the article is in a journal to which your library does not subscribe. Fortunately, however, even when a full-text version of the article is not available to you online and your library does not have the journal in question, the interlibrary loan department can usually obtain a copy of the article for you in relatively short time. In addition to journal articles, don't forget the "hidden literature" (essays or chapters on the topic that are parts of books rather than printed in journals). The *Essay and General Literature Index* (online or the bound volume) is essential for this purpose. The footnotes and endnotes of the articles and essays you locate should also be examined for possible further additions to your bibliography.

Once you have reduced your sources to a manageable number (in this case, the guidelines called for a maximum of 20 titles), you are ready to read and take notes. You must necessarily approach your reading somewhat differently from what you would do for an ordinary term paper, where you are reading in order to extract information about the topic itself. Remember, your focus should be on what the historians are doing. In order to extract this kind of information, it is necessary to read the sources with the purpose of the essay in mind: to inform the reader about some of the major writings on the topic, about how these works differ from one another, and about how the historiography evolves over time. Titles, as we have seen, usually give us some idea of the author's plan. As we saw in Chapter 4, examining tables of contents, prefaces, introductions, and conclusions is another way to get a quick fix on an author's orientation. If you do this before actually reading the work (and it is not always necessary to read every work in its entirety), you will be much better able to look for and find especially significant passages, which reveal the author's approach or methodology. As you do so, take notes on 5 × 8 or 4 × 6 inch note cards, and don't forget to include precise page references to passages you may wish to cite or quote. The same care must be given to making full and precise note cards of your reading as to compiling your bibliography card file. It is also possible to take notes on your computer; but, if you do so, you must devise a good method of grouping entries that relate to the same topic. There are software products on the market that facilitate this. One clear advantage of computerized notes is that, when you are writing the paper, it is easy, if you have taken good notes, to copy and paste for quotations. You may, however, find that filling out cards by hand turns out to be simpler and quicker. While the computer makes both bibliographic searching and writing vastly more efficient than the old methods, its advantage when it comes to notetaking is by no means so clear-cut.

Writing the Historiographic Essay

Now we can turn to the writing of your historiographic essay on this subject. It is crucial to remember that this paper will not be a history of the Lewis and Clark Expedition, but rather an account of how historians have written about the topic. Of course, a number of facts concerning Lewis and Clark will be introduced into the essay, but they are used to illustrate the approaches and findings of the various authors. When writing a historiographic essay, a good method is to think of yourself as preparing a guide to the historiography for a fellow student, who knows a little about the period but has a very limited knowledge of the topic. The introduction to the paper can therefore provide some facts about the Lewis and Clark Expedition in order to remind or inform the reader of some of its basic features. Consider how the opening paragraphs in Patricia Autran's historiographic essay establish this foundation and conclude with a "bridge" to the discussion of the historians who have written about Lewis and Clark – which forms the body of the paper. Note that quotations from the secondary sources being discussed are either set off by quotation marks or, for longer passages, given in "block quotation" (or "extract") form, without quotation marks. Some quotations of less than a sentence are grafted onto the author's sentence, making a "run-in" quotation. These types of quotations, along with other aspects of the essay, are pointed out in the marginal comments. (For more on quotations, see the section on quoting in the next chapter). Further observations on how this essay is constructed follow the essay, and also appear in the marginal comments. You will find endnote references immediately following the text of the essay.

Introduction
providing the basic
facts about the Lewis
and Clark Expedition

"Ocian[1] in View! O! the joy."[2] These words were written on November 6, 1805 by the jubilant William Clark upon reaching the goal of one of the most dramatic undertakings in American history. Long before the acquisition of the Louisiana Territory in 1803, President Thomas Jefferson had begun planning for the exploration of this enormous area that no American citizen had ever traversed. Jefferson, who had long been fascinated by the unknown territory, hoped that the exploration would lead to the discovery of a river route capable of carrying trading goods from the Mississippi River to the Pacific Ocean. The Louisiana Purchase facilitated the enterprise and gave the president a sense of urgency about beginning the exploration as soon as possible. Captains Meriwether Lewis and William Clark[3] led the Corps of Discovery on an exciting and hazardous journey, which began in May 1804 and lasted 28 months, ending with their return to St. Louis in September 1806.

In addition to discovering a water route from the Mississippi to the Pacific, the expedition had several other important purposes. Lewis and Clark were to make a complete scientific survey of the regions along the route of the Missouri River, across the Rocky Mountains, down the Columbia River, and finally to the Pacific Ocean. They were to determine the longitude and latitude of the area, analyze and describe plant and animal life, and report on the culture of the native peoples they encountered. Most importantly, they were asked to evaluate the possibilities of trade and agriculture in that region.

During the journey, Lewis and Clark produced eight detailed volumes, whose content ranged from maps, climate, geography, and ethnic observations to descriptions of new species of plants and animals. Their journals also included a dramatic day-by-day story of the adventures and hardships experienced by the group. The information contained in them would be studied and analyzed for the next two centuries. Historians produced many books, articles, and essays using the material from these volumes. Over time, each writer has interpreted and approached the history of the Lewis and Clark Expedition in a different manner and each has attempted to meet a particular historiographic goal.

Although the writing of the expedition's history began *Transition to* soon after the volumes were released, this essay will focus *discussion of* on those works produced during the last half century or *historiography of the* so. Most of the serious scholarly studies were undertaken *topic* after the end of World War II. In the 1940s, most of the writings are of a general, narrative nature. John Bakeless, in his 1947 book *Partners in Discovery*,[4] offers an overall description of the great adventure. He begins with the planning of the expedition, continues with the dramatic details of the exploration, and ends by discussing the aftermath and results of the enterprise. His narrative tells the story of the expedition in a very thorough and clear manner. The author is deeply impressed by the explorers' achievements, though he considers Lewis to have often been rash and reckless in his judgments. Bakeless's book is considered one of the first satisfactory accounts of the Lewis and Clark Expedition[5] and it provided a foundation for later scholars. It also reflects the confident, even triumphalist mood of the United States following World War II.

In the same year when Bakeless's book appeared, Jay *Transition to next* Monaghan produced a lengthy essay entitled "Lewis and *author* Clark." Monaghan begins his account when Lewis was a boy and Jefferson first had thoughts of a westering exploration. He approaches the story in an individualistic manner, attempting to give the reader the background of each participant and to humanize them, so that the reader may better understand how and why the events took place. Monaghan tries to establish the view that Lewis may have been "born" for this adventure, that it was destiny: "He was also a seeker of knowl- *Short quotation* edge like Jefferson himself."[6] His account differs from the previous ones in that, as well as retelling the story of the expedition, it touches on political motives and gives significant credit to the other members of the

Corps, stating that each played an important role and had a unique personality. In his analysis of the various personalities, Monaghan highlights the importance of the psychological interplay between the expedition's members. Monaghan even mentions York, Clark's Negro slave who went along on the difficult trip. York would become a subject of interest to future historians, as would Sacagawea, the Indian woman who played a role in the success of the expedition. Monaghan describes her participation as well.

By the 1950s, historians began to take a deeper look into not only the adventurous aspects of the expedition, but the impact that the exploration had on the development of the United States. In 1952 Bernard DeVoto, who also edited a selection of the Lewis and Clark journals,[7] published a book called *The Course of Empire*. Since DeVoto's book is on western exploration generally, the Lewis and Clark Expedition forms only a part of his story, yet he devotes considerable space to it. Like previous historians, DeVoto points out its romantic and adventurous aspects, noting that "one who spends time reading the records of wilderness men is in danger of taking for granted the labor, strain, hardship, weariness, hunger, thirst, passion, fear, anger, pain, desire and wonder that were their fare."[8] Yet DeVoto also stresses the importance of this expedition by connecting it to Jefferson's goal of establishing an empire of liberty: "Here was the Great South Sea, the Pacific Ocean and they had brought the United States to its shore."[9] With this, he implies the major impact that the expedition had on the future success of the United States. Most importantly, DeVoto calls attention to the fact that many technical aspects of the Lewis and Clark Expedition had been neglected and needed further comprehensive study. This observation led to a richer historiography of the expedition, as writers began to look more into the achievements of the Corps of Discovery in the field of natural history.

Transition to next author

Responding to this perceived need for greater attention to the Corps' scientific achievements, Raymond Darwin Burroughs released his book *The Natural History of the Lewis and Clark Expedition* in 1961.[10] Burroughs approached his history in a very scientific manner. Following a brief narrative of the expedition in the introduction, the rest of the book is quite technical. He divides it into chapters named after the animals that were discovered and studied by Lewis and Clark during their journey: bears, raccoons, weasels, wild dogs and cats, and bison. Lewis and Clark are credited with being the first to give reliable descriptions of wildlife in this area. Throughout his book, Burroughs stresses the importance of analyzing thoroughly the natural discoveries made by the expedition and their impact on scientific study.

Paul Russell Cutright, in his 1969 book *Lewis and Clark:*   *Transition to next*
Pioneering Naturalists, successfully accomplishes the goals set   *author*
by both DeVoto and Burroughs.[11] Like them, he calls attention
to the neglect of the technical aspects of the Lewis and Clark Expedition
among historians. Cutright offers what he believes to be the reason for the
neglect of the scientific aspects of the expedition, claiming that the slighting
of the scientific phases had its inception almost immediately after Lewis and
Clark concluded their historic journey. Thomas Jefferson, early in 1807,
appointed Meriwether Lewis to the post of Governor of the Territory of
Louisiana instead of allowing him to devote all his energies and talents to
writing a compendious narrative, which would encompass the scientific discoveries of the expedition. The appointment was an illusory reward and a
consequential error, as Jefferson would soon learn. Cutright goes on to explain
that Lewis died an unexpected death and that the volumes were edited by
other writers, who left out much of the natural history. Cutright, a biologist,
meets his objectives by presenting a careful assessment of the expedition's
scientific accomplishments. He focuses on botany, zoology, geography,
anthropology, and medicine. His book contains many historical facts about
the events and the people involved, but these facts revolve around his main
purpose of presenting to the reader the major scientific contributions made
by Lewis and Clark. He concludes each chapter with a summary of the discoveries within each area traversed by the Corps.

Interest in the scientific aspects of the expedition did   *Transitional*
not end with Cutright, but rather continued after him with   *paragraph to works*
an even deeper focus. The often harrowing facts concern-   *dealing with the*
ing the health of the expedition members seem almost   *medical history of the*
fictional in nature. It is nothing short of a miracle that all   *expedition*
but one of the original members survived the long and
dangerous exploration of the Wild West. Several writers were intrigued by
this fact and were compelled to study and write about it. Now the history of
the Lewis and Clark Expedition would take on a medical turn.

The medical aspects of the expedition came to the fore in a 1971 article
entitled "Lewis and Clark: Westering physicians."[12] The author, Drake Will,
employs a narrative style, but his story revolves strictly around the health,
illnesses, and treatments of the exploring party. Will's introduction includes
portions of a letter written by Thomas Jefferson to Dr. Benjamin Rush of Phila-
delphia, asking Doctor Rush to prepare some notes for Captain Lewis. These
notes were to include several medical questions about the native people and
some directions for the preservation of Lewis's health as well as the health of

the other members of the Corps. Will goes in detail through the various illnesses experienced by members and informs the reader about the remedies and treatments that were used by both Lewis and Clark throughout the journey. Interestingly, he even explains the medical events involved in the birth of Sacagawea's baby, Pompey. Nor did Will omit the fact that the men of the Corps purchased moments of passion from the native women and consequently contracted venereal diseases. He also mentions the fact that Lewis and Clark were for the most part very skeptical of the medical practices of the native people, even though at times they reported the apparent success of those practices.

Continuing the emphasis on the medical history of the Lewis and Clark Expedition was Eldon Chuinard, a medical doctor, in his 1979 book *Only One Man Died*. It is not surprising that Dr. Chuinard would be fascinated by the fact that, although not one licensed physician accompanied the Corps of Discovery on this dangerous expedition, only one man failed to survive. In the introduction Dr. Chuinard mentions a comment made by

Ellipsis to show   Bernard DeVoto in his book *The Course of Empire* to the
omitted material at   effect that the medical aspects of the expedition had
end of sentence   received little attention. To this comment Chuinard replies: "To this author this subject is interesting and important; and it has been my effort in this book to exhaust the subject without exhausting the reader [...]."[13]

Dr. Chuinard states his objectives clearly in the introduction:

> This book is not meant to be another general and complete review of the story of the Expedition. Terrain, climate, geography, biology, botany, and the commercial aspects are muted, being mentioned to orient the reader in time and place, and mainly for the purpose of indicating their effects on the health of the men [...] only enough of the geography, climate, edibles, and Indian customs are excerpted from the journals to indicate the health problems that the Expedition faced in certain locations and conditions [...] therefore the scope of medical reference is considerably more extensive than the recounting of specific diseases and their treatments.[14]

Block quotation above   The author writes about the medical practices of Lewis and Clark and credits them with considerable success in the treatment of the expedition's members. Dr. Chuinard believes that, although the captains were not physicians by profession, "they were truly great physicians in native ability and devotion."[15] Chuinard includes lists of medicines that were purchased for the journey. He describes the illnesses and treatments that were experienced by all the members and devotes an entire chapter to Indian medicine. His amazement that the expedition accomplished all of the president's requests while losing only one man is evident throughout his book.

Yet another writer interested in the scientific aspects of the journey was the geographer John Logan Allen. In his 1979 book *Passage through the Garden: Lewis and Clark and the Image of the American Northwest*, Allen examines the expedition's geographical achievements. After exhaustively analyzing every map, narrative, and scrap of information that the explorers had at the start of their journey, the author is able to present a clear picture of their mental image of the region. He then shows how their discoveries altered this image and shattered many erroneous beliefs, such as that the Rockies were of the same height as the Appalachians. This profusely illustrated volume allows the reader to gain a much clearer sense of the changes brought about by the expedition in the field of geographic knowledge.[16]

Some historians have focused their attention not on the expedition as a whole or on some aspect of it such as medical care, but rather on its two heroic leaders. This biographical approach to the topic can be seen in Richard Dillon's 1965 book *Meriwether Lewis*. Dillon's main *Transition to discussion of works with a biographical focus* purpose in writing the biography was to consider Lewis in isolation from the expedition, and especially from Clark, so that the reader might better understand the "one man who deserves to be considered as the person who opened up the Far West." Dillon seems *Run-in quotation* adamant about persuading the reader away from thinking of Lewis as only one half in the partnership with Clark, and he is critical of the failure of previous writers and historians to focus on each of the expedition's leaders individually: "Both Lewis and Clark have suffered from this shotgun marriage of convenience, brokered by lazy historians more content with image than reality."[17] Dillon attempts a full reappraisal of Lewis, who, he argues, was much more important than Clark to the success of the expedition. Dillon calls attention to two characteristics of Lewis that, in his opinion, are often unnoticed. The first is Lewis's narrative abilities, demonstrated in the writing of his national epic. The second characteristic is Lewis's superior ability as a diplomat among the Indian nations.

The other half of the famous duo has not been ignored by biographers. In 1977, Jerome Steffen published his study of William Clark. The book, entitled *William Clark: Jeffersonian Man on the Frontier,* provides information about Clark's early years as well as about his post-expedition accomplishments. Steffen suggests that Lewis may have been given more credit than he deserved in regard to the scientific success of the Corps of Discovery: "The expedition provided an intellectual opportunity for a man who, from boyhood, had demonstrated a deep interest in natural science and history. Clark made innumerable scientific contributions to the expedition, many usually attributed to his partner."[18] Unlike Dillon, Steffen is not anxious to study Clark in isolation from Lewis. His goal is to identify William Clark as an eighteenth-century Enlightenment figure.

The historiography of the Lewis and Clark Expedition has been enriched by the perspectives of the histories of ethnic minorities, which have developed over the last few decades. The complex relationship between the expedition members and the native peoples they encountered was, until the 1960s, only lightly covered. In the earlier works discussed in this essay, the Indians were mentioned only in a general manner and for the purpose of glorifying the civilized ways of Lewis and Clark. In the medical aspects of the expedition's history, the Indians tend to be blamed for soldiers' venereal diseases.

Transition to works focusing on Native Americans

A deepening interest in the native people of the West emerged as early as 1966, when John Ewers published an article called "Plains Indian reactions to the Lewis and Clark Expedition." For the first time, the history of the expedition was interpreted from a native perspective. Ewers explains that the encounter of these Indians with Lewis and Clark was by no means their first encounter with whites. By the time of the expedition the Indians had been trading with them for quite some time. For the most part, Indians were suspicious of whites. They were not ignorant of the interest that white men had in them and in the resources of their country. Despite this, the Indians' overall reaction to Lewis and Clark was fair. Ewers concentrates his study mostly on the Mandan Tribe. He does this because Lewis and Clark spent several months near the Mandan villages and these Indians had a greater opportunity to get to know the explorers. Ewers goes into detail about the relationship between the Mandan Indians and the explorers. For the most part, the Mandans regarded Lewis and Clark in a friendly manner, but the author concludes that, in the field of diplomacy, the expedition was not as successful as in other fields. He claims that the reactions of the Indians to Lewis and Clark were of historical importance: "The reactions of these Indians to their meetings with Lewis and Clark were important to the future relations of United States Citizens with the native peoples of an area larger than that of the original thirteen states."[19]

James P. Ronda continued the line of emphasizing the Indian encounters with the expedition. His book *Lewis and Clark among the Indians* was released in 1984. Ronda's purpose in writing it was to shift the focus of the history of the expedition to Indian–white encounters in North America. This approach is symptomatic of a tendency, during the last two decades, for historians – especially those writing on the history of the Americas – to dispense with the concept of heroic "discovery" by white men and to recast events as a series of "encounters." Ronda makes it clear, from the beginning, that his book is not another general review of the famous expedition. He concentrates on the daily dealings of the Indians with the Corps of Discovery and gives much detail about the customs and culture of the Indians: "In the simplest terms, this book is about what happens when people from different cultural persuasions meet and deal with each other."[20] He gives much credit to Lewis and Clark for the gathering of information on natives that has helped historians to better understand the culture of the Indians during this period. Ronda credits himself with filling a gap in the history of the Lewis and Clark Expedition and with offering a fresh approach as well. He shares Ewers's view that, overall, the expedition failed in point of diplomacy toward Indians. Ronda makes a final statement about the important role the Indians played in the success of the exploration. Furthermore, he points to the presence of Sacagawea in the group as a key to understanding just how important the support of the natives was to the survival of the explorers.

Even before Ronda's book appeared, historians had begun to look in detail at this intrepid Indian woman. In *Sacagawea of the Lewis and Clark Expedition* (1979), Ella Clark and Margot Edmonds tackled the controversy over Sacagawea's true role in the expedition. Popular but unfounded beliefs about the brave and beautiful Indian woman had her single-handedly guiding the large group through unexplored territory and dying as an old woman in Wind River, Wyoming, in 1884. While demonstrating that neither of these beliefs is supported by the evidence, the authors do relate in considerable detail the significant contributions of Sacagawea to the expedition. Their biography is an attempt to clarify the truth about the "myths," as they call them:

Block quotation below

> It is the aim of this biography to place Sacagawea's life and accomplishments in historical perspective, and to dispel the fog of idolatry which has surrounded her for so long. Our intention is not, as might be supposed, to depreciate what she did or to lessen her role in the Lewis and Clark Expedition. On the contrary, we hope to emphasize her importance by plainly stating the part she played in a historic feat.[21]

The first part of the book tells the story of Sacagawea's role in the Lewis and Clark Expedition, while the second part covers her life following the expedition. It seems natural that Sacagawea would become a focus of attention for historians in the 1970s, at a time when the fight for women's equality and recognition was prominent and women's history had emerged as a significant area of study.

Transition to works on African American members of the expedition

Another member of the expedition whose role was in need of clarification was York, William Clark's slave. The attention paid to York is certainly connected to the emergence of African American history as an important field during the past few decades. Robert B. Betts makes an attempt to clarify this element of background in his 1985 book *In Search of York*. As with Sacagawea, it was York's fate that many myths were created about his role in the expedition. He has been portrayed as a tall, strong man who contributed only entertainment in the form of comedy to the rest of the Corps and had an amicable relationship with his master. Betts boldly claims: "How this came about is in itself a cameo example of the way our history was for so long presented from an almost exclusively white point of view […]." He continues by stating the primary purpose of his book, which is "to break through the stereotype and try to see York as a credible human being, a man who knew firsthand his country at its best and its worst – from the heights of magnificent achievement of the exploration to the depths of slavery."[22] Betts accomplishes his goal by offering details about York and his participation in the expedition. He obtained most of this information directly, from what was written about York in the journals. Betts makes it no secret that he is disappointed in the failure of historians, both black and white, to take seriously this forgotten slave – who in his opinion made important contributions to the expedition.

Run-in quotation

Several works on the expedition published during the 1990s, partly under the influence of postmodernist interest in deconstructing historical "discourses," focus on the language employed by members of the Corps in their letters and journals. In his book *Acts of Discovery: Visions of America in the Lewis and Clark Journals*, published in 1993,[23] Albert Furtwangler examines the

Transition to recent works, some of them postmodernist, dealing with the writings of the expedition

Lewis and Clark Expedition as history, literature, and science. Furtwangler, a specialist in American literature, argues that the journals are not simply primary-source materials for historians, but should also be considered an important literary work. He is more interested in the idea of discovery and in how this idea evolved in the minds of Lewis and Clark during their journey than he is in the external events of the discovery. The author is especially concerned with how Lewis and Clark fashioned new modes of expression to convey their encounters with new terrain, people, animals, plants, and foods.

In 1994 Gunther Barth examined the impact of the expedition's journals in his article "Timeless journals: Reading Lewis and Clark with Nicholas Biddle's help." Barth reviews the publication history of the journals of the expedition, focusing in on the contributions of Nicholas Biddle, who was the author of *History of the Expedition of Captains Lewis and Clark*, published in 1814. He begins with an overview of the expedition and notes that Biddle, not Lewis or Clark, was the main source of knowledge about the enterprise throughout the nineteenth century. Biddle chose to downplay any elements of doubt or confusion in the captains' behavior and to ignore all references in the journals to topics like sex and venereal disease. The resulting journals, expurgated and sanitized, presented, according to Barth, a grand, heroic narrative that suited the nationalistic needs of nineteenth-century Americans and changed the expedition's leaders into "taciturn classic heroes."[24] Continuing this interest in closely analyzing the language of the explorers, in 1997 Frank Bergon published an article titled "Wilderness aesthetics." Bergon praises Lewis and Clark for their "fresh, flexible uses of the vernacular," which anticipate writers like Thoreau; but his overall assessment is critical: "In portending the destruction of one

Combination of run-in quotation with one set off by a colon

civilization and the rise of another, the journals reveal the dark, imperialistic underside of the epical adventure."[25]

The most recent among the books discussed here is also the most impressive: Stephen E. Ambrose's *Undaunted Courage: Meriwether Lewis, Thomas Jefferson, and the Opening of the American West* (1996). A comprehensive account of the background and details of the expedition, Ambrose's book resembles some of the much earlier works in its celebration of courage. The author examines Lewis's close and enduring friendship with Thomas Jefferson and shows how faithfully Lewis reflected the president's passionate interest in the commercial potential as well as in the scientific discoveries of the expedition. The overall tone is adulatory, and Ambrose does not accept Bakeless's negative assessment of Lewis. He does admit that Lewis mishandled several crises in the wilderness, but he considers these to be occasional and uncharacteristic lapses of judgment. Putting these missteps into context with Lewis's alcohol problem and with his suicide several years later, Ambrose suggests that he was probably a manic depressive.[26] The author takes fully into account the recent, more specialized scholarship on the expedition, making this highly readable book a skillful work of synthesis as well as a careful study based on primary-source materials.

Concluding paragraph notes the overall evolution of the historiography and anticipates future interest in the topic

Over the years, since Meriwether Lewis and William Clark led the Corps of Discovery across the uncharted wilderness to the Pacific Ocean and back, the achievements of their expedition and its significance for America have been carefully studied. The earlier emphasis on the journey as an epic of courage and heroism has, throughout the years, evolved historiographically into more tightly focused analyses and interpretations, involving such topics as natural discoveries, medicine, geography, and perspectives based on the history of Native Americans, women, and blacks. The recent postmodernist interest in deconstructing historical narratives has also attracted scholars to the topic. Scholarly interest in the Lewis and Clark Expedition shows no sign of fading. Rather it is likely to increase with the approach of the bicentennial of the expedition and with the release of the final volumes of the most complete and accurate scholarly edition of the Lewis and Clark Journals ever published.[27]

Endnotes

#1 content endnote

1   An example of the eccentric spelling employed by both Lewis and Clark.

2 Quoted in Stephen E. Ambrose, *Undaunted Courage: Meriwether Lewis, Thomas Jefferson, and the Opening of the American West* (New York: Simon & Schuster, 1996), 310.

#2 indicates primary-source material quoted from second source

3 Actually only Lewis held the rank of captain. Clark was still a lieutenant. However, Lewis insisted that they were co-commanders, and the enlisted men,

#3 combination of content and reference note

believing them to be of equal rank, addressed them both as "Captain." Ambrose, *Undaunted Courage*, 134–6.

4 John Bakeless, *Lewis and Clark: Partners in Discovery* (New York: William Morrow & Company, 1947).

5 According to *Readers' Guide to American History* (Boston, MA: Houghton Mifflin, 1991), 402.

6 Jay Monaghan, "Lewis and Clark," in Jay Monaghan, *The Overland Trail* (Indianapolis, IN: Bobbs-Merrill Company, 1947), 34.

7 Bernard DeVoto, ed. *The Journals of Lewis and Clark* (Boston, MA: Houghton, Mifflin, 1953).

8 Bernard DeVoto, *The Course of Empire* (Boston, MA: Houghton, Mifflin, 1952), xvii.

9 DeVoto, *The Course of Empire*, 553.

#9 Subsequent

10 Raymond Darwin Burroughs, *The Natural History of the Lewis and Clark Expedition.* (East Lansing, MI: Michigan State University Press, 1961).

reference to previously cited work (more than one work by author)

11 Paul Russell Cutright, *Lewis and Clark: Pioneering Naturalists* (Urbana, IL: University of Illlinois Press, 1969).

12 Drake Will, "Westering physicians," *Montana History* 21.4 (1971): 2–17.

13 Eldon Chuinard, *Only One Man Died: The Medical Aspects of the Lewis and Clark Expedition* (Glendale, CA: Arthur H. Clark Company, 1979), 26.

14 Chuinard, *Only One Man Died*, 27–28.

#14 & 15 subsequent

15 Chuinard, *Only One Man Died*, 31.

references to

16 John Logan Allen, *Passage through the Garden: Lewis and Clark and the Image of the American Northwest* (Urbana, IL: University of Illinois Press, 1975).

previously cited work (only one work by author)

17 Richard Dillon, *Meriwether Lewis: A Biography* (New York: Coward-McCann, 1965), xiii.

18 Jerome Steffen, *William Clark: Jeffersonian Man on the Frontier* (Norman, OK: University of Oklahoma Press, 1977), 6.

19   John Ewers, "Plains Indians reactions to the Lewis and Clark Expedition," *Montana History* 16.1 (1966): 2.

20   James P. Ronda, *Lewis and Clark among the Indians* (Lincoln, NE: University of Nebraska Press, 1984), xi.

21   Ella Clark and Margot Edmonds, *Sacagawea of the Lewis and Clark Expedition.* (Berkeley, CA: University of California Press, 1979), 2.

22   Robert B. Betts, *In Search of York* (Boulder, CO: Colorado Associated University Press, 1985), 6.

23   Albert Furtwangler, *Acts of Discovery, Visions of America in the Lewis and Clark Journals* (Urbana, IL: University of Illinois Press, 1993).

24   Gunther Barth, "Timeless journals: Reading Lewis and Clark with Nicholas Biddle's help," *Pacific Historical Review* 63 (1994): 515.

25   Frank Bergon, "Wilderness aesthetics," *American Literary History* 9 (1997): 133, 159.

26   Ambrose, *Undaunted Courage*, 312.

27   Gary E. Moulton, ed. *The Journals of the Lewis and Clark Expedition*, 13 vols. (Lincoln: University of Nebraska Press, 1983). The final volumes of this edition are scheduled to be published by 2003.

Bibliography

Allen, John Logan. *Passage through the Garden: Lewis and Clark and the Image of the American Northwest.* Urbana, IL: University of Illinois Press, 1975.

Ambrose, Stephen E. *Undaunted Courage: Meriwether Lewis, Thomas Jefferson, and the Opening of the American West.* New York: Simon & Schuster, 1996.

Barth, Gunther. "Timeless Journals: Reading Lewis and Clark with Nicholas Biddle's help." *Pacific Historical Review* 63 (1994): 499–519.

Bakeless, John. *Lewis and Clark: Partners in Discovery.* New York: William Morrow & Company, 1947.

Bergon, Frank. "Wilderness aesthetics." *American Literary History* 9 (1997): 128–61.

Betts, Robert. *In Search of York.* Boulder, CO: Colorado Associated University Press, 1985.

Burroughs, Raymond Darwin. *The Natural History of the Lewis and Clark Expedition.* East Lansing, MI: Michigan State University Press, 1961.

Chuinard, Eldon G. *Only One Man Died: The Medical Aspects of the Lewis and Clark Expedition.* Glendale, CA: Arthur H. Clark Company, 1979.

Clark, Ella, and Margot Edmonds. *Sacagawea of the Lewis and Clark Expedition.* Berkeley, CA: University of California Press, 1979.

Cutright, Paul Russell. *Lewis and Clark: Pioneering Naturalists.* Urbana, IL: University of Illinois Press, 1969.

DeVoto, Bernard. *The Course of Empire.* Boston, MA: Houghton, Mifflin, 1952.

Dillon, Richard. *Meriwether Lewis: A Biography.* New York: Coward-McCann, 1965.

Ewers, John. "Plains Indian reactions to the Lewis and Clark Expedition." *Montana History* 16.1 (1966): 2–12.

Furtwangler, Albert. *Acts of Discovery, Visions of America.* Urbana, IL: University of Illinois Press, 1993.

Monaghan, Jay. "Lewis and Clark." In Jay Monaghan, *The Overland Trail.* Indianapolis, IN: Bobbs-Merrill Company, 1947.

Ronda, James P. *Lewis and Clark among the Indians.* Lincoln, NE: University of Nebraska Press, 1984.

Steffen, Jerome O. *William Clark: Jeffersonian Man on the Frontier.* Norman, OK: University of Oklahoma Press, 1977.

Will, Drake. "Westering physicians." *Montana History* 21.4 (1971): 2–17.

It will be noted that the concluding paragraph sums up the major approaches that have been taken by historians of this topic since the end of World War II. It also reminds the reader of the approaching bicentennial and suggests that considerable scholarly activity on this topic should be expected in the next few years. Since the bicentennial of the expedition (2004) has come and gone, anyone undertaking such an essay presently would obviously have to pay heed to major recent works of scholarship, such as Jeffrey Ostler's *The Plains Sioux and US Colonialism from Lewis and Clark to Wounded Knee* or William R. Swagerty's *The Indianization of Lewis and Clark.*[2] It might also be possible,

2 Jeffrey Ostler, *The Plains Sioux and US Colonialism from Lewis and Clark to Wounded Knee* (Cambridge: Cambridge University Press, 2004); William R. Swagerty, *The Indianization of Lewis and Clark* (Norman, OK: Arthur H. Clark Company, 2012).

depending on the guidelines of your essay, to include some film source, such as Ken's Burns's excellent 1997 TV documentary *Lewis and Clark: The Journey of the Corps of Discovery*.

Note that, in the historiographic essay, endnotes rather than footnotes were used. If the specifications for the paper had called for footnotes, these would have been placed at the bottom of each page (this is done automatically by selecting "footnotes" rather than "endnotes" in your word processor). Use arabic numerals for notes. If the footnote/endnote menu on your word processor happens to be set to roman numerals, change the setting to arabic. The bibliography should come last. Also, every page of the essay, including the bibliography, should be consecutively paginated (use the pagination function of your word processor). It is customary to leave the first page of text unpaginated. An unpaginated cover sheet should also be attached, giving the title of the paper, your name, course information, instructor, and date.

Alternative Approaches

Because we considered Ms. Autran's essay as a good example, it should not be imagined that the structure and style of all historiographic essays must conform to it. There are other successful methods of writing this kind of essay. It will be noted that in our example the author chose to organize the material chronologically – that is, proceeding from the first book discussed (published in 1947), through succeeding years up to the late 1990s. Alternatively, she might have employed a topical approach in which, for example, all biographical works, or those concerned with the scientific activities of the expedition, would be discussed in succession, regardless of their date of publication. The chronological approach usually works best, but there is no rigid formula. Whether the approach is topical, chronological, or some combination thereof depends on many factors, not least on the author's preference.

Regardless of the approach you choose to take, a number of valuable insights should emerge from the writing of a historiographic essay. For one thing, it is an especially valuable device for developing and honing your library research skills. Even more importantly, it encourages, indeed compels, the reading of history with an eye to understanding the approaches and methods of various historians. It enables you to think historiographically, an essential attainment for those who are serious about understanding history as an intellectual discipline. It also puts one in an excellent frame of mind for undertaking a major research paper – an operation we will examine next.

7

Engaging with Primary Sources

The Research Paper

In the last chapter we examined some effective methods of researching and writing the historiographic essay; now we will consider the same process for the research paper. The former is concerned almost entirely with secondary sources, while the latter is informed by all available primary sources as well as by the relevant secondary works. Moreover, a research paper is usually longer than a historiographic essay. The first true research paper most undergraduates undertake is the senior thesis – a substantial project sometimes extending over an entire academic year, often under the auspices of a seminar. A term paper prepared for an upper division history course may sometimes be extensive enough to qualify as a research paper, although it is usually shorter and based on relatively few sources. Still, many of the skills and methods requisite for the longer project will be quite applicable to the term paper as well.

A senior thesis or a similarly extensive research project can be considered a capstone experience for an undergraduate major in history. It brings together the knowledge and insights gained

Going to the Sources: A Guide to Historical Research and Writing, Fifth Edition.
Anthony Brundage.
© 2013 John Wiley & Sons, Ltd. Published 2013 by John Wiley & Sons, Ltd.

from previous courses, one's recently acquired research skills, and one's growing powers of analysis, imagination, and expression. It offers the opportunity to move beyond a somewhat passive mode of learning into the critical and analytical mode of the self-directed research scholar. Approached with the proper attitude of adventure and determination, it can prove to be the most valuable and memorable academic experience of one's undergraduate career.

Searching for a Viable Topic

As was the case with the historiographic essay, the first step to writing a successful research paper is to settle upon a topic of manageable scope – a process that, again, almost certainly requires some pruning down of the first subject you select. There are, however, considerations that are peculiar to the research paper. For example, it is usually necessary to choose a topic for which a significant quantity of primary-source material is accessible to you. By checking on the availability of published sources (or even of close-at-hand manuscripts that you know you are allowed to use) early on in the research process, you can avert a potentially large waste of time. Otherwise, diligent research in the library catalog and in various indexes might yield an admirable array of secondary works, but few if any primary sources. It is possible, of course, that the nature of the topic or your instructor's guidelines would render a paucity of primary sources acceptable, but be sure to check.

At this point one might object that I have drawn too tight a distinction between primary and secondary sources. Is it not the case that the authors of books, articles, and essays often quote freely from primary materials? And, in writing a research paper, is it not perfectly acceptable to use, and even quote, the sources used by other historians? After all, the amount of primary-source material that could be gathered in this fashion from a couple of dozen secondary works might be considerable. The answer is that, while it is acceptable to quote material quoted by others, this should be done sparingly and not as a substitute for reading through and selecting from a much larger mass of primary sources. The rule is always to use the fullest, best edited collection of any primary source available to you. Under this rule, the most "nutritious" source would be the unedited manuscripts, or the editions of those sources in which the manuscripts are reproduced in their entirety. From there there is a descending scale, along which the sources used are more and more highly processed (as in *The Selected Letters of. . .*). Primary-source material quoted in a secondary work is usually only a fraction of the body of material from which it was selected. In dealing with primary sources, the historian's task is to select representative and illustrative documents from as large a collection as possible. Becoming a sensitive, skillful, and efficient analyst of source material is a vital part of training to be a historian.

Finding Primary Sources

Since we explored the process of finding secondary works in the last two chapters, we can concentrate here on the process of locating primary sources. One method that was mentioned earlier – a method for finding collections of documents in book form – is to look under the various subject headings for your topic in the library catalog to see if there are any with the word "sources" added. If you are working on a biographical topic, or if your topic has significant biographical components, look for the name(s) of the major person(s) in your historical account both under author and under subject entries. A keyword search on a person should lead you to both. Anything written by any of your historical players is a primary source.

Another effective method is to look for published bibliographies on your topic, which may be in the form of essays or articles as well as in the form of books. Some of the major places to find the titles of published bibliographies are the subject heading catalog and the *Guide to Reference Books* edited by Balay (see Chapter 3). Many published bibliographies that you locate through any of these means will have a section on primary sources. Most will have a much larger chronological or topical sweep than your topic, and you will need to look up your time period or topic in the table of contents or index. A good example is the *Harvard Guide to American History*, an excellent reference source for primary and secondary sources, though it is a bit dated for the latter.[1] If you are working on some aspect of the American Revolution, for example, looking under that section in the *Harvard Guide* will refer you to several useful collections of published documents. You may also wish to investigate the availability of local manuscript sources and whether or not your library has an oral history collection.

In searching for published collections of primary sources, consult the bibliographies and footnotes of your secondary sources, as well as doing some creative shelf browsing. In many historical monographs the bibliographies at the end of the book are divided into primary and secondary sources. The former section is sometimes further subdivided into manuscript and published sources. In articles and essays, be sure to mine the footnotes for references to published sources. As for shelf browsing, it can be quite effective with regard to primary sources, especially if you are still at the stage of searching for a topic. If, for example, you decided you would like to do a research paper on modern India but had not refined the topic beyond that, your scanning of the library stacks on the history of India might reveal the massive, multivolume *Collected Works of Mahatma Gandhi*. The availability of this source could serve to point you toward a manageable topic, one that would probably but not necessarily be biographical in nature.

Finally, if the period you are studying falls in the last century or so, you may want to research newspapers or periodicals contemporary with the events you are studying. The *Times* (London) and the *New York Times* are widely available on microfilm, and your library's reference room should have indexes that will allow

---

[1] Revised edition, edited by Frank Freidel (Cambridge, MA: Belknap Press, 1974). This, by the way, is another example of a "split footnote."

you to access these newspapers for material on particular topics or persons. In some libraries, these and other papers are searchable online. Many other newspapers are also available, both on microfilm and as bound volumes, but their indexes usually do not go back before the 1970s. This need not preclude the use of unindexed newspapers; for, if you are looking for items about particular events for which you know the dates, you can search the newspapers published immediately following the events. In regard to magazine articles from the period you are investigating, *Poole's Index* and the *Readers' Guide to Periodical Literature* (*Readers' Guide Full Text* and *Readers' Guide Retro* online) will open up the riches of nineteenth- and twentieth-century periodical publications of a more popular bent.

Approaching Your Reading

It is unnecessary, indeed unadvisable, to defer reading until you have accumulated your entire list of sources. As was noted in the last chapter, it is a good idea to begin reading something immediately, so as to gain some command over the basic factual details and to get assistance in refining the scope of your topic. It is best to begin your reading with the secondary works, because without some factual grasp of the topic you will not be able to analyze the primary sources effectively. Also, it is necessary to be aware of some of the historiographic dimensions of your subject before you finish reading. This entails following the kind of procedure discussed in the last chapter for a historiographic essay. When you have gained an understanding of the kinds of questions posed and of the approaches taken by other historians, you will be much more skillful in your own encounters with the primary sources.

By no means should it be thought that I am advising a "hands-off" policy on primary materials until all the secondary works have been digested. To begin with, such a stern counsel would be hypocritical, since I never observe it myself. On the contrary, whenever I undertake a new project, I can hardly wait to get my hands on the primary sources. Moreover, it would not be a good idea to observe a rigid order of reading. When writing a research paper, you will be involved in two processes: (1) extracting information from the secondary works as well as analyzing them historiographically; (2) reading through a variety of primary sources, both for information and for quotable material. These two processes, if not quite simultaneous, are at least interwoven. Thus, while questions are fresh in your mind from reading another historian's account, it is a good time to plunge into the primary sources. Sudden, unexpected insights and connections can occur when you vary your reading in this fashion.

Another advantage of making an early foray into primary materials is that many of them are direct, vivid, and dramatic. Alternating them with books, articles, and essays of other historians is a refreshing change of pace and an excellent device for maintaining a high level of interest in your subject. The same applies to your reading of secondary works. Do not feel that you must plod through one weighty tome cover to cover before you can start reading another. There is no reason why you should not be working on several books at the same time. The main thing is not to adopt an overly rigid methodology. It is important to keep a fresh, lively attitude and to enjoy the process. Experiment with different ways of doing your reading until you find one that works best for you.

Notetaking

As you read, always have a stack of 5 × 8 or 4 × 6 note cards or your computer next to you. Lined index cards are not essential – pads of paper of this size work quite well. (The 3 × 5 cards used for bibliographies are too small for effective notetaking.) Many students and not a few scholars prefer to take research notes in spiral notebooks, but doing so has a number of drawbacks. Notes kept in this fashion (on consecutive pages) might work well enough for the relatively few sources consulted in a typical term paper, but, in all but the most expert hands, this format tends to prove restrictive and inefficient for larger projects. The major drawback is the lack of flexibility. With a notebook you will not be able to group and regroup notes relating to the same subtopic. When the time arrives to write a particular portion of your paper, a very frustrating search through the notebook would be required. The same problem can apply to notetaking on your computer, unless you establish a good indexing system or you use software designed for the purpose.

Note cards, on the other hand, can be quickly and easily segregated into stacks on the basis of the facet of the subject to which they refer. Even if you divided your notebook into sections for each subtopic, it would still be inflexible, for it frequently happens that, after the research for a project is completed, you decide to divide the subject into a quite different set of subtopics from what you originally planned. If all your notes are in a notebook, you will be confronted with the problem of turning back and forth to find notes on each of your new subtopics. With cards, it is supremely easy – you simply reshuffle them to correspond to your new subtopics or ideas. Also, you can rearrange the sequence of cards relating to each subtopic to make them reflect the sequence of points you plan to make in your paper. Another advantage is that a quick glance at the size of each stack of cards can indicate whether you need more material on a certain subtopic, should merge it with another, further subdivide it, or perhaps drop it altogether.

Cards should be kept in some kind of file box, preferably with tabbed file separators dividing the cards for each subtopic. It is also a good idea to place some kind of identifying word or mark on the top line of each card, to facilitate filing after a notetaking session. Also, if all your cards have subtopic headings, they can be quickly resegregated should they ever be dropped or scattered. Beyond this minimal identifying mark (which might be simply a letter or a number) there should be a brief description on the first line, allowing you to tell the contents at a glance without having to read it all. This will save a good deal of time when you start writing, or if you decide to rearrange the cards due to a change from your original plan.

Having considered the mechanics of notetaking, let us turn to the substance of the process. Students are often baffled as to how many notes they should take, and of what types. Should you record each and every "fact" you read? If so, your stack of note cards would swell to unmanageable proportions before you finished reading the first book, and you would doubtless begin to experience writer's cramp, if not total burnout. You will encounter a tremendous amount of factual detail about your topic in your reading, most of which does not warrant the time and effort for a note. In the course of reading a large number of historians' accounts as well as primary sources, you will acquire a familiarity with the major events, processes, and persons that constitute your subject. Take notes only on those facts that you have reason to think will be necessary in your later analysis of the subject and in the writing of the paper. On the other hand, being too sparing in your notetaking will leave you with a paucity of material when the time to write arrives. Obviously it is a question of acquiring a sense of balance, something that comes with practice.

Putting certain facts on cards for later retrieval and analysis is only one of the purposes of notetaking. Another is to record the views of other historians regarding your topic. These might be described as historiographic notes. Remember that in your research paper you will not only illuminate your topic through the use of primary sources, but you should also explain to your readers, at least to some extent, the historiographic dimensions of the topic. Another purpose is to record those primary sources, or some portion of them, that you think you may want to quote or cite in your paper.

Finally, you should take notes of your own thoughts and reflections as you read. This is part of the creative process in research. Perhaps some comparison suddenly occurs to you, or you think of a particular way in which you would like to analyze certain documents when you get around to writing the paper. Do not count on remembering these insights later. Write them down, either on separate cards or as bracketed inserts on the cards containing notes on the material in question. It is also an excellent idea to keep a separate small notebook for the purpose of recording your more general, overarching ruminations, and to make notes to yourself about things to be researched, verified, or further explored later.

At this point perhaps it is best to illustrate the process of note-taking by quoting a note of my own. The project in question was research for a book on John Richard Green, who, you may recall from Chapter 1, is the author of the very influential *Short History of the English People* (1874). In that part of my research dealing with the impact of the *Short History*, I came across an article written just after Green's death by a scholar who had worked with Green during the latter's tenure as a Church of England clergyman. I was struck by one passage and filled out the following note card:

Popularity of Short History

"When men leaving Oxford wished to improve their minds, if they were rich they traveled, and if they were poor they read Green's Short History."
Philip Lyttleton Gell, "John Richard Green," Contemporary Review
39 (1883): 738.

Several points should be observed about this note card. Since it was written by a contemporary and a friend of Green's, it is a quotation from a primary source. In fact, it is from an obituary article on Green. I took down the quotation partly because it had a nice ring to it and was "atmospheric," that is, it nicely conveyed the tone and style of the Victorian intellectual circles in which Green moved. The card's heading tells me at a glance what the card is about and allows it to be filed with other cards on the same subtopic. I also took care to cite the source and page number for this quotation. My actual card has only the notation "Gell (1883), 738," since I already had a bibliography card for this article, with a complete citation. Note, however, that I also included the date (1883) in this citation, allowing this source to be distinguished from any other works by the same author that might be in my bibliography. To be on the safe side, it would be a good idea to add a short title to distinguish this source from other works by Gell, in case he had published two or more in 1883.

It is also quite a short note, and it might be thought that the vacant space on the card could be used for other notes. This, however, would violate a cardinal principle of notetaking: only one fact, thought, idea, or quotation per card. To do otherwise is to undermine the flexibility of the card system. The final thing that should be said about this card is that I did not end up using it. When I got around to writing the book,[2] I decided, somewhat reluctantly, to omit it. The focus of the chapter in which I had planned to use it had changed from my original intent, and the quotation seemed peripheral and unnecessary. You will almost certainly take a good many more notes than you will actually use in the writing of the paper, but this is inherent in the scholarly process. A thoughtful, judicious selection of material from your reading should be followed by a thoughtful, judicious selection from your own notes when the time comes to write.

The Outline and Structure of Your Paper

Well before you have finished your research and are ready to write, you should begin developing an outline of your paper. It is important to give this matter some thought even at the start of your research. Although any outline you come up with at this point will necessarily be tentative and undeveloped, it will nonetheless launch you into the process of thinking structurally and will help you to direct your research efficiently. As with all papers, the major divisions of the research paper are the introduction, the body of the paper, and the conclusion. It is with the outline of the body of the paper that you should chiefly concern

[2]   Anthony Brundage, *The People's Historian: John Richard Green and the Writing of History in Victorian England* (Westport, CT: Greenwood Press, 1994).

yourself. Initially you will simply be blocking in a few major topics, but, as you continue to read, think, and take notes, your outline will develop accordingly. Your outline should in fact continue to be amended even as you enter the writing phase. One of the most counterproductive postures you can adopt is to imagine that your outline is at some stage chiseled on stone tablets. You must be free at any time throughout the process to adopt changes, sometimes of major proportions.

The fully developed outline is the blueprint for the sequence of paragraphs that will constitute your paper. Just as the various topics and subtopics in the outline are related to paragraphs and clusters of paragraphs in the paper, they are also related to the note cards you are filling out, arranging, and classifying. Your note cards, in fact, are an important key to developing an effective outline. When each note card is filled out, there is a brief entry on the top line describing the contents. When cards dealing with the same thing are aggregated, they provide one of your topics or subtopics. The number of notes in each group will tell you how much material you have on each subtopic and will suggest to you if further subdivision is needed. It may be that you have only a few notes on a particular subtopic, which presents you with a decision about whether to do additional research in that area, merge that subtopic with another, or perhaps drop it altogether. Each time this happens, you should amend your outline accordingly.

A recognition of the interrelationship between your clusters of notes and the items on the outline will help you keep some sense of balance and symmetry to your project. But an outline does not simply reflect the noted material you have accumulated. It should also be a sequence of topics and subtopics, each one of which leads smoothly into the next. That is, your outline establishes a structure for the natural and graceful set of linkages that the completed paper should exhibit. A careful look at your evolving outline can alert you to harsh disjunctions and allow you to rearrange sequences to permit an easy transition from one topic to another.

Some Elements of Effective Writing

"Always start at the beginning" may not be the best advice to offer someone engaged in a research paper. In many cases, the introduction is best left in a relatively incomplete state until the body of the paper, and possibly even the conclusion, is completed. As we have seen, it is very likely that the focus of the topic will shift somewhat, not only during the research phase but even during the writing. Nonetheless, a couple of functions of a good introduction should be noted. First, it should clearly inform the reader about the nature and scope of the paper. It should also include something on the basic historiographic dimensions of the subject, along with an indication of the approach you are taking. Another important function of a good introduction is to engage the reader's interest. Clarity is always an excellent means to this end. Some writers start with a vivid passage describing a central event or process, in order to create atmosphere and draw the reader into the topic, before going on to describe the scope of the paper. This is not appropriate in all cases, but for many topics such a "hook" can provide an effective beginning.

An impressive use of this device can be seen in the opening paragraphs of *The Crucial Decade*, the late Eric F. Goldman's classic study of the United States following World War II. Consider how powerfully the author creates the atmosphere of 1945 in a few deft narrative paragraphs:

A US Radio monitor in a little frame house in Oregon caught the first hint. The Japanese were interested in peace, the Domei broadcast said, provided that the prerogatives of the Emperor would not be "prejudiced." Then came two days of diplomacy, a few hours of false armistice, more waiting through an interminable weekend. Finally, on Tuesday, August 14, 1945, reporters were summoned to the Oval Office of the White House. President Truman glanced at the clock to make sure he was holding to the agreement of simultaneous announcement in Washington, London, and Moscow. At exactly 7 p.m. he began reading: Late that afternoon a message had been received from the Japanese Government which "I deem [...] full acceptance of [...] unconditional surrender."

Across America the traditional signs of victory flared and thousands snakedanced in a pouring rain and a St. Louis crowd, suddenly hushing its whistles and tossing aside the confetti, persuaded a minister to hold services at 2 a.m. New York City, hardly unaccustomed to furor, amazed itself. With the first flash of V-J, up went the windows and down came the torn telephone books, the hats, bottles, bolts of silk, books, wastebaskets, and shoes, more than five thousand tons of jubilant litter. Whole families made their way to Times Square until two million people were milling about, breaking into snatches of the conga, hugging and kissing anybody in sight, greeting each twinkle of V-J news on the Times electric sign with a cheer that roared from the East River to the Hudson. The hoopla swirled on into the dawn, died down, broke out again the next afternoon, finally subsided only with another midnight.

Americans had quite a celebration and yet, in a way, the celebration never really rang true. People were so gay, so determinedly gay. The nation was a carnival but the festivities, as a reporter wrote from Chicago, "didn't seem like so much. It was such a peculiar peace. [...] And everybody talked of 'the end of the war,' not of 'victory.'" The President himself spoke with a mixed tone. When the crowds around the White House chanted: "We want Harry," he appeared beaming with Bess on his arm and proclaimed this "a great day." His face quickly sobered as he added warnings of an "emergency ahead – a crisis as great [...] as December 7, 1941." At V-J, 1945, the United States was entering the newest of its eras in a curious, unprecedented jumble of moods.[3]

Goldman not only gives us vivid narrative here, he also delineates the atmosphere of 1945 and hints at its complexity. Criticisms of this type of approach as being too "popular" or "journalistic" are sometimes made. In response, it might be said that, among the various possible reactions to reading Goldman's introductory paragraphs, closing the book seems the least likely.

[3]   Eric F. Goldman, *The Crucial Decade and After: America, 1945–1960* (New York: Vintage Books, 1961), 3–4.

Acquiring and maintaining a reader's interest should be a high priority for all historians, not just in the introduction but throughout the work. It is true, of course, that many topics do not readily lend themselves to the kind of anecdotal treatment just described. It is also true that telling a story well is only a part of the historian's calling. Imposing pattern and meaning on a jumble of events is the historian's central task. This often requires a tone of dispassionate analysis and the use of generalization and abstraction rather than the relating of an exciting narrative. Obviously, any portion of your work can either be well written or poorly written. While your readers should not expect you to keep them "entertained" throughout your work, they do have the right to as much incisiveness, clarity, and wit as you can at all times muster.

Attention to mechanics (like an effective outline) has an obviously beneficial effect on your written work. A clear, straightforward structure in which each section is designed to lead naturally into the next is essential. Things are not quite so clear when it comes to effective style. Here we are dealing with matters such as syntax and word choice, in which many different "correct" choices are possible. Furthermore, writing style is, or should be, as distinctive as personality. One way your writing is sure to undergo improvement, however, is through the active and critical reading of many well-written histories. By taking care to note how other authors structure their works and deploy language effectively, you can gain insights into your own writing.

There are, of course, some frequently cited injunctions, such as avoiding the use of long, convoluted sentences or of short, choppy ones, and especially a long succession of sentences of the same length. Such admonitions, however, are qualified. The judicious use of the complex or very brief sentence enlivens your writing and is a relief to the eye and ear. All stylistic "rules" are only general guidelines, which the confident writer will not hesitate to ignore when the occasion demands. There are some sound practices that enhance word choice, such as a ready resort to the dictionary and thesaurus. One of the major ways to improve your writing style is to be willing to undertake multiple revisions of your work. It is often said that "writing is rewriting." Whatever the level of your expressive abilities and the facility with which you write, there is no substitute for careful editing and reworking, a process we will consider in more detail later in the chapter.

An Open Mind and Intellectual Honesty

Apart from effective structure and style, concerns shared equally by writers in all subjects, there is an issue with which historians at any level should be especially concerned: intellectual honesty. I am not suggesting that there is any widespread problem of historians consciously setting out to deceive their readers or to distort the truth. I am talking about making a determined effort to be genuinely impartial in selecting, analyzing, and presenting the evidence. Most of us like to think of ourselves as impartial and fair-minded, but deploying this attitude to good effect in research and writing is not as simple as it sounds. Even if a topic is new to us, we usually start with some slight knowledge of it and some interpretation of it, however hazy and unformed. This, indeed, is a good starting point. At an early stage of your research, ask yourself such questions as: What do I know about this subject and what do I consider its significance to be? What views do I have about the motives of the major decision-makers involved? What impact did the events and people I will be dealing with have on subsequent history? Jot these questions down and return to them periodically, as a method of guarding against the unconscious tendency of looking for – and seeing – only that evidence that bolsters your preconceptions. As you research and reflect, consider as many alternative answers to your questions as possible.

Just as we must guard against partiality in selecting evidence, the same care must be taken in analyzing it. Primary sources need to be treated with respect as well as with skepticism. If, like a trial lawyer or a debater, you proceed as though you were involved in an adversarial process, you will end up amassing only that evidence favorable to your side, and then torturing its meaning to fit a desired outcome. Remaining open-minded is crucial to being an effective researcher; it also helps ensure that your ideas and your work will develop in exciting and unanticipated ways. This is not to say that historians should avoid assertiveness in their interpretation of events, or should refrain from debates with other scholars. As we have seen, it is precisely these characteristics that make history the lively, dynamic, and valuable discipline it is. What is crucial is that our firmly held convictions be the result of our scholarly labors, and not a set of prejudices resolutely fortified by our turning a blind eye to contrary or even unpleasant evidence.

Quoting

As mentioned, one commonly observed characteristic of student research papers is that they are too heavily laden with quotes. There are no doubt many reasons why student authors tend to bolster their work with the words of others. The least charitable explanation is that it seems an expeditious way of filling the requisite number of pages for the paper; but I doubt that this accounts for more than a handful of cases. More common is the notion that generous chunks of primary-source material will, in addition to functioning as evidence, impart atmosphere to the paper. This is sometimes the case, but only if the material is evocative, well stated, and appropriate. Even then, the rule should be to quote only as much of a passage as is necessary, without destroying or distorting the meaning of the longer document from which it is excerpted. Otherwise you should simply describe or paraphrase the contents of the document. Overly lengthy or ill-chosen quotations impede the text and tire the reader. Quotations should never be allowed to become roadblocks in the smooth flow of historical narrative and analysis.

With these caveats in mind, let's consider some of the mechanics of quotation. When you find a passage you think you might like to use in your paper, fill out a note card, or make a computer entry, indicating the precise reference to the source. If you are uncertain just how much of the quote you will be using, play it safe and note an extended passage. You can decide later about how much of it to insert into your paper. Often you will find that you want to use various portions of a document and that they are separated by material extraneous to your purpose. In this case you can omit the unwanted material, provided that: (a) by your omission you do not distort the meaning of the entire passage, or that of the larger context in which it appears; (b) you indicate, through the use of ellipsis points, that material has been omitted.

Examples of the use of ellipsis points (or simply ellipsis, "omission") – three evenly spaced periods – are to be seen in the introductory paragraphs of Eric Goldman's *The Crucial Decade*, quoted above. When Goldman tells of President Truman's announcement of the Japanese surrender, he quotes only one sentence and prunes it considerably, so that it flows into his narrative. Truman described the message from the Japanese Government: "I deem [...] full acceptance of [...] unconditional surrender." A couple of paragraphs later, again, Goldman uses ellipsis to good effect in quoting the words of a Chicago reporter: "It was such a peculiar peace. [...] And everybody talked of 'the end of the war,' not of 'victory.'"

In the first passage the omitted material, indicated by the two sets of ellipsis points, is within a single sentence. In the second passage we know that the omitted material is more than one sentence, because there is a period immediately after the word "peace" and before the ellipsis points. Note also that the word "And" is capitalized, indicating that in the original source it is the beginning of another sentence. Did Goldman meet the other requirement of the use of ellipsis points, namely that the omission of material not distort the meaning of the document? Only a check of the full sources he used can answer that question. But it is easy to see how very distorted the meaning of the original would have been had the author left out the final phrase of the Chicago reporter's second sentence, so that it read: "And everybody talked of 'the end of the war' [...]" This would be an accurate quotation, and ellipsis points would be correctly used; but eliminating the phrase "not of 'victory'" utterly confounds and obscures the original meaning.

Ellipsis points are a most helpful device, allowing the use of only those portions of a document that are of interest to you. They permit a very flexible tailoring of the quoted material, so that it meshes with your writing without impeding the narrative flow. This smooth integration of primary material with your work is easiest when the material quoted is brief – a sentence or less. There are times, of course, when you need to quote lengthier passages, perhaps as much as a paragraph or so. This is bound to impede the flow of your work at least slightly; but, if you are satisfied that it will enhance your paper, you should have no compunctions about quoting it.

If the quotation is only a couple of sentences, you can simply set it off with a colon and quotation marks. For passages that are going to exceed four or five lines, you should use a block quotation, in which the passage is single-spaced and indented from the left and right margins. With a block quotation quotation marks are not used, since it is clear from the additional indentation and single spacing that material is being quoted. (As you have probably noticed, this book is riddled with block quotations.) A quotation of a page or more – a device to be used very sparingly – is often best placed in an appendix to your paper.

Footnoting

We can divide our discussion of footnoting into what needs to be footnoted and how it should be done. In regard to the former, most students are fully aware that all quotations must be footnoted; it is the actual footnoting of other material that raises problems. Should each "fact" be footnoted? To do so would be to encumber your text with thick clusters of numbers and a corresponding long list of notes at the bottom of each page (or at the end of the paper, if endnotes are being used). The purpose of footnoting is to allow your reader to check on the accuracy of your quotations, citations, and assertions. You should not footnote a major fact that is well known and unchallenged, such as "President Lincoln was assassinated by John Wilkes Booth" or "The Normans invaded England in 1066." Nor is it necessary to footnote most of those "smaller" facts about events or details in a person's life that the reader can easily check by consulting some of the works in your bibliography. But when such a fact is being emphasized or used as evidence, and certainly when it is in dispute, it needs to be footnoted. Also use a footnote when mentioning another work, primary or secondary, in your text, even if you do not quote from it directly.

There are two basic types of footnotes (or endnotes): reference footnotes and content footnotes. The former documents a quotation, citation, or assertion that cites the bibliographic information on the source, including the page number (if applicable). This is the most common type of footnote; and your major concern with it is to format it correctly. There are several major style manuals, and it is important to find out which one (if any) your instructor recommends, then to stick to it consistently. *The Chicago Manual of Style* is the most commonly used in the historical profession,[4] but be sure to check with your instructor. The note format used determines such matters as the manner and sequence in which publication data are stated, how subsequent references to the same work are made, and so on.

The content footnote requires some explanation. One use of it is to provide further elaboration on some point made in a paper without encumbering the text with a digression that may be of only marginal interest to some readers. Digressions in a story are sometimes unavoidable and can be highly interesting, but if they are employed too often the reader's patience and attention will begin to wane. It is like listening to a long-winded speaker who

---

[4]   See *The Chicago Manual of Style*, 16th ed. (Chicago, IL: University of Chicago Press, 2010). A shorter, cheaper, and much more convenient reference work for accessing the University of Chicago format is Kate L. Turabian, *A Manual for Writers of Term Papers, Theses, and Dissertations*, 7th ed. (Chicago, IL: University of Chicago Press, 2007).

insists on giving you a wealth of background detail about each component of his story. We not only grow weary, but such meanderings become so distracting that we lose track of the point and direction of the story. One of the advantages of the written over the spoken word is that such collateral material can be consigned to a content footnote where, perhaps in a few sentences or in a paragraph, additional information can be imparted to any reader who may be particularly interested in that point. By using a content footnote correctly, you allow the body of the text to remain unencumbered.

A similar use of the content footnote is that of providing a brief historiographical discussion on some point without cluttering the text. You may, for example, want to relate some fact over which a few scholars are in dispute, or offer differing interpretations. This may be combined with a reference footnote; that is, a citation to a source in your footnote might be immediately followed by something like: "However, this view has recently been challenged by X, who introduces new evidence that casts some doubt on the genuineness of the draft treaty. See..." (here you would have the complete citation to the revisionist article by X).

Whether you are inserting a reference or a content footnote, be sure to use the footnoting function of your word processor. If you neglect to use the footnote command and simply type footnote numbers directly into the text, you will deprive yourself of a very significant advantage of your word processor – its ability to keep track of footnote numbers and of their relation to the corresponding notes by changing the numbers automatically whenever you eliminate or rearrange a footnoted passage. None of us, with experience of writing in the pre-computer era, are likely to forget how quickly manually inserted footnote numbers could get out of sync with the notes, necessitating laborious and time-consuming corrections. Ascertain that the footnote settings on your word processor are correct for the kind of note – footnote or endnote – that you are going to use. Also ensure that you have clicked on the option for arabic, not roman numerals (1, 2, 3, not i, ii, iii). And insert the text of the note as soon as the footnote window opens on your screen. If you put that part of the process off until later, you will have to spend additional time finding the book, article, or note card that you need to cite.[5]

Editing and Revising

If you are striving for excellence in your written work, there is no substitute for painstaking editing and revising. No matter how good you may feel about the quality of your first draft, a later critical scrutiny is certain to reveal inconsistencies, abrupt transitions, unclear passages, infelicitous expressions, and other matters in need of urgent attention. To a lesser degree, the same will apply to a perusal of your second draft, as well as to a third. Rewriting is a critically important phase of the scholarly process, not something that might be squeezed in if you have enough time left before the deadline for submitting your paper. Time is always in short supply for the harried student, so it is essential to plan its use wisely. In addition to leaving time for rewriting, you should, if possible, allow for some "percolation time" – a few days away from research, writing, and rewriting, in which your thoughts can percolate and fresh insights can emerge. It is especially valuable to leave some time between the writing of drafts of your paper and the final version.

As you go over your first draft, it is useful to read it aloud. This brings your ear into the process, allowing you to detect more easily those passages that need remedial attention. This is also very helpful in proofreading, because, when we reading our own work silently, we tend to see what we expect to see and we can miss omitted or duplicated letters or words. Having a fellow

---

[5]   What has just been said about the need to use the footnoting system of your word processor can be extended to other functions. Take some time to learn the capabilities of your word-processing application before you start writing – it will pay big dividends. An example is the tendency to use the tab (tabulator) key or space bar for indenting paragraphs instead of the formatting commands of the word processing application. When tab indentations or spaces are used, any subsequent change in font, font size, margins, or other formatting features can wreak havoc with the appearance of the text.

student listen as you read your work aloud (or read it aloud to you) can also be useful, as long as you have reason to believe that he or she has the ability, interest, and candor to comment critically. Sometimes a senior thesis is taught on a seminar basis, in which portions of rough drafts are read by one's fellow students, who then offer constructive criticism to one another (in addition to that of the instructor). Such encounters almost invariably prove rewarding and interesting, and they create a strong atmosphere of mutual support. These seminars are, or can be, microcosms of the "communities of scholars" that exist in the wider historical profession.

The number of drafts you write will depend on many factors, including your writing abilities, the time at your disposal, and the views of your instructor. Fortunately the computer has made this part of the writing process immeasurably speedier and more efficient. Once the body of your paper is in good shape, you can turn your attention to revising the introduction and conclusion – for now you know exactly what it is that you need to introduce and to conclude.

The introduction should set forth, clearly and briefly, the scope of your paper, the main points to be covered, and a brief statement of your thesis. It is always desirable to engage the reader's attention as quickly as possible, and a well-crafted introduction is the key. This may, as mentioned, involve the use of a "hook" (a vivid incident, illustrative of the events you are about to relate in your paper). It should usually involve a brief historiographic discussion, giving the reader some sense of how the scholarship on your topic has evolved. It should always involve clear sentences, effective structure, and other elements of good writing.

The careful crafting of your conclusion is equally important. Here the emphasis should be on reminding the reader of the main points you have covered, without recapitulating the details of the story. More importantly, here is where you present your overarching conclusion(s) about the material. Don't overreach on the conclusion. Look honestly at the evidence you have marshaled, and ask yourself if it supports the conclusion(s) you have in mind. Remember that most historical evidence is open to a variety of interpretations, some more compelling than others. A sweeping interpretive statement that forecloses all other possibilities may have a resounding ring to it, but it is apt to be a red flag to any reader aware of the complexities, ambiguities, and nuances of history. Make your conclusion as strong as the evidence and the structure of your argument warrant, but don't push it beyond that point.

Finally you need to add the bibliography, which comes at the very end of the paper. Your instructor will probably have some guidelines for the bibliography, but it is a common practice to present a list of the primary sources first, followed by a separate listing of the secondary sources. Make sure the entire document is paginated consecutively from the first page of text (page number 1) to the last page of the bibliography. (The page number should not be printed on the first page of text, an option available in most word-processing applications.) Page numbers should be inserted on all other pages (by using the pagination command of your word processor), including the "back matter" – the endnotes (if endnotes are used instead of footnotes) and the bibliography. Make a final spelling check of the entire document, and then go ahead and print it. You should also prepare and print an unpaginated cover sheet with your name, the title of your paper, the course, the instructor, and the date.

One Final Look

Now that you have given the print command and everything seems to be in order, there is a natural desire to slap the paper into a nice-looking binder and present it to the instructor as quickly as possible. Resist the temptation. Treat what you have before you as a final rough draft. If you have a few days before the due date, lay it aside and give yourself a little extra "percolation time." Then go back to it and read it through, carefully and aloud, with a critical eye and ear. You are certain to note some rough spots in the text, and probably some formatting irregularities and other problems. You want to present the very best work you are capable of, and you should also want it to look as good as possible. Taking pride in both the content and the appearance of your work is the hallmark of the professional in any field. Do not sell yourself short by neglecting this final opportunity for improvement.

8

Conclusion

The Open-Ended Nature of History

In legal instruments known as articles of apprenticeship, which were commonly used in medieval and early modern England, the description used to refer to an occupation to which a young person was being apprenticed was "art, science, craft, or mystery." This phrase conveys the sense that there were important expressive and creative components even to the most mundane lines of manufacture in the preindustrial age. It is a phrase peculiarly appropriate for the historian's calling. However much the practice of history seems to involve the systematic application of certain skills, there are wide, important areas of both research and writing that call upon the creative spirit. Recall that the Greeks considered history an important enough expressive field to assign one of the nine Muses to it. The modern historical profession still embraces this traditional identification as a branch of literature, even though it often functions in close alliance with the social sciences, or indeed is sometimes classified as one of them. Far from being troubled by their discipline's duality, most

Going to the Sources: A Guide to Historical Research and Writing, Fifth Edition.
Anthony Brundage.
© 2013 John Wiley & Sons, Ltd. Published 2013 by John Wiley & Sons, Ltd.

historians glory in it. The point is that, whether history is viewed as one of the humanities or as one of the social sciences, its creative dimensions are of central importance.

In the sections of this book dealing with research and writing, the emphasis has been on matters that might be considered mechanical in nature – the use of library catalogs, indexes, and various electronic resources, as well as some techniques of reading, notetaking, writing, and revising. One reason for this emphasis is the absolute necessity for students to be well grounded in historical methodology. Another is, quite frankly, that it is much easier to examine systematically the elements of good historical craftsmanship than it is to explain creativity. There are no rules or techniques for being creative, and few creative people in any field can offer much in the way of guidance. Hunches, sudden insights, and inspirations are some of the undoubted manifestations of creativity, but one is tempted to place them in the realm of "mystery," as people did in medieval times.

Even if, ultimately, creativity cannot be explained, it is possible to recognize it, to encourage it, and to extend it. The first and essential thing is to discard the notion that a charmed minority of individuals are naturally creative, while everyone else is forever doomed to being a plodder. Whatever mental and psychological processes are involved in creativity, they are – allowing for inevitable differences in capacity and intensity – possessed by everyone. It is possible, of course, for people to convince themselves, or to allow others to convince them, that they are somehow deficient in intelligence and imagination. Others may be persuaded that it is not prudent to display any creative qualities. In many societies, past and present, creative impulses are viewed with suspicion, out of fear that they may pose a threat to the established order and ways of doing things. Certain religious systems, ideologies, and political programs, insofar as they claim to possess a monopoly on truth, are also inhospitable to the creative spirit. Historical writers with a burning sense of having the mission to advance particular causes almost invariably subvert the skeptical, open-minded characteristics of the discipline, which are essential if creativity is to flourish. It is a central function of education generally, and of universities in particular, to counter-act these baneful tendencies.

One of the best ways historians can aid in this endeavor is to insist on the open-endedness of their discipline. It has been one of the purposes of this book to set forth a view of history as dynamic and evolving. Our views of the past evolve as we move into the future and thus acquire an ever-changing vantage point. Like travelers toiling up the side of a mountain, we find that the configuration of the landscape behind us has changed each time we turn around. Features that were once prominent recede into obscurity while others loom into view, and new patterns and relationships can be discerned. A shifting panorama is, after all, one of the things that make a journey interesting and instructive. It is all too possible, alas, to take a journey without looking around, or to do so in such a cursory fashion that nothing of significance is detected. No one sets out to write a dull, plodding account; one of the best ways to avoid doing so is to keep in mind that even the smallest project of historical inquiry is part of a larger intellectual odyssey.

My insistence on linking creativity with a conception of history as open-ended perhaps raises the old troubling question about whether or not there is such a thing as objective truth. If "everything is relative," what can we really know about the past? If history is simply a product of the imagination, then is not every person's version as "true" as another's? The answer is a resounding no. Of course there is objective truth in history; it may be elusive, but it is usually accessible; and it must always be rigorously pursued. Truth in history resides in those ascertainable facts that make up the superstructure of any historical account. Whether or not King Harold of England perished at the hands of Norman invaders in the so-called Battle of Hastings in 1066 can be determined by marshaling every fragment of the surviving evidence, by assessing each source for its authenticity and reliability, and by noting inconsistencies and contradictions. The result of this process is an overwhelming conviction that indeed Harold was killed on that eventful October day. His death has become duly registered as one of those countless facts that constitute the annals of the past. Of course, in some sense it, like any fact, must be considered provisional, that is, subject to being changed should contradictory evidence come to light. Nonetheless, it remains a remarkably "sturdy" fact that, like the vast majority of other verifiable occurrences, will almost certainly not be altered. Thus we can rest assured that these verified past events will not be plucked away or overturned by whim or fancy.

But, contrary to popular belief, the broad array of widely accepted facts does not constitute history. History is the intellectual discipline that, in addition to discovering, verifying, and describing past events, imposes pattern and meaning upon them. Indeed, the imposing of pattern and meaning and the discerning of processes are the most important parts of the historian's calling. It is here that creativity flourishes. Here, too, is the arena in which historians offer fresh approaches, new methodologies, and sometimes major revisionist interpretations. If history is conceived as a fixed chronicle, there is little scope for either creativity or revisionism, which march hand in hand. And historians must continue to offer these things if history is to respond to the changing needs and aspirations of the ever-advancing present, as well as to provide thoughtful anticipation of the future.

Appendix A
Published Bibliographies

Guide to Reference Books. Edited by Robert Balay. 11th ed. Chicago, IL: American Library Association, 1996. In the section on history, this guide lists numerous bibliographies and other reference materials (atlases, chronologies, etc.) for all facets of historical study.

Bibliographies in History. Foreword by Eric H. Boehm. 2 vols. Santa Barbara, CA: ABC–Clio, 1988. Volume 1 lists published bibliographies on US and Canadian history; volume 2 covers all other countries.

American Historical Association's Guide to Historical Literature. Edited by Mary Beth Norton. 3rd ed., 2 vols. New York: Oxford University Press, 1995. An excellent guide to essential books, articles, and essays in all fields of history.

Harvard Guide to American History. Edited by Frank Freidel. Rev. ed. Cambridge, MA: Belknap Press, 1974. Though a bit dated, this is still a useful guide to both primary and secondary sources.

Historiography: An Annotated Bibliography of Journal Articles, Books, and Dissertations. Edited by Susan K. Kinnell. 2 vols. Santa Barbara, CA: ABC–Clio, 1987.

People in World History: An Index to Biographies in History Journals and Dissertations in All Countries of the World except the US and Canada. Edited by

Going to the Sources: A Guide to Historical Research and Writing, Fifth Edition. Anthony Brundage.
© 2013 John Wiley & Sons, Ltd. Published 2013 by John Wiley & Sons, Ltd.

Susan K. Kinnell. 2 vols. Santa Barbara, CA: ABC–Clio, 1988. A very full and useful index by occupation, region or country, as well as surname.

People in History: An Index to US and Canadian Biographies in History Journals and Dissertations. Edited by Susan K. Kinnell. 2 vols. Santa Barbara, CA: ABC–Clio, 1988. A very full and useful index by occupation, region, and surname.

Reference Sources in History: An Introductory Guide. 2d ed. Edited by Ronald H. Fritze. Santa Barbara: ABC–Clio, 2004. A helpful guide to a wide range of reference materials in history.

Appendix B
Major Databases for Bibliographic Searching

The following are widely available, most of them in both online and published form, a few only in published volumes. New databases are certain to be added, while others are apt to undergo at least partial name changes. You should always explore any interesting-sounding database in your quest for sources.

WorldCat
ArticleFirst
Humanities Index (called Humanities Full Text in its online form)
Social Sciences Index (called Social Sciences Full Text in its online form)
Essay and General Literature Index
Historical Abstracts
America: History and Life
Academic Search Elite
World History Full Text
OmniFile Full Text Mega
JSTOR
Dissertation Abstracts International
Hispanic American Periodicals Index
British Humanities Index

Going to the Sources: A Guide to Historical Research and Writing, Fifth Edition.
Anthony Brundage.
© 2013 John Wiley & Sons, Ltd. Published 2013 by John Wiley & Sons, Ltd.

Appendix C
Footnote/Endnote Formatting

The following examples employ the University of Chicago style, which is most commonly used in the historical profession. These examples cover the great majority of citations required.

Books

A book citation in a footnote/endnote requires: (a) the author's name as given on the title page (first name first); (b) full title (including subtitle, if any); (c) place of publication, publisher, and date (usually in parentheses); (d) page number(s) of the specific citation, unless it is the entire work rather than some part that is being cited. In addition, if the book cited is an edition other than the first, this must be indicated following the title (e.g. "2d ed."). If no place of publication or date of publication is given, insert "n.p." or "n.d." In a multivolume work, the volume number

Going to the Sources: A Guide to Historical Research and Writing, Fifth Edition.
Anthony Brundage.
© 2013 John Wiley & Sons, Ltd. Published 2013 by John Wiley & Sons, Ltd.

must be indicated just prior to the page numbers if you refer to a specific part of the work. If the citation is to the entire work, give the number of volumes (e.g. "3 vols.") immediately after the title. In the Chicago style, page number citations for book chapters are not preceded by "p." or "pp." In all styles, titles of books are always italicized, not placed in quotation marks. This convention differs across cultures (e.g. in German or Italian books), but it is invariably the same in all English-language books.

Book by a single author

1   Andrew Cunningham McLaughlin, *America and Britain* (New York: E. P. Dutton, 1919), 137.

Book by two authors

2   Fritz M. Heichelheim and Cedric A. Yeo, *A History of the Roman People* (Englewood Cliffs, NJ: Prentice-Hall, 1962), 296.

Book by three authors

3   Richard Hofstadter, William Miller, and Daniel Aaron, *The American Republic* (Englewood Cliffs, NJ: Prentice-Hall, 1959), vol. 2, 391.

NOTE   This is an example of a specific citation from one volume of a multivolume work.

Book by four or more authors

4   James Henretta and others, *America's History*, 4th ed., 2 vols. (New York, NY and Boston, MA: Bedford/St. Martin's, 2000).

NOTE   This is an example of (1) the citation of an entire multivolume work; (2) the citation of a later edition. When works by four or more authors are listed in the bibliography, however, all the authors' names need to be included.

Book with author(s) as editor(s)

5   Donald T. Critchlow and Charles H. Parker, eds., *With Us always: Private Charity and Public Assistance in Historical Perspective* (Lanham, MD: Rowman & Littlefield, 1998).
    NOTE   This is how to cite an entire book of essays (chapters) written by various authors. (The proper formatting for individual essays is given below.)

Articles and Essays (Chapters)

The styling of the authors' names (including in multiple authorship) is the same as for books. The titles of articles are normally in quotation marks, and they are never italicized. The names of journals and other periodicals are always italicized. The volume number of a journal follows immediately after the journal name, most often without "vol.," "v.," or other such designations. This number is usually followed (in parentheses) by the date of the specific issue of the journal volume. A colon and page numbers follow. If the entire article is being cited, the numbers should represent the inclusive page range of the full article. If just a portion of the article is being cited, only the corresponding page number (or numbers) should follow.

Journal article

6   Thomas Benjamin, "A time of reconquest: History, the Maya revival, and the Zapatista rebellion in Chiapas," *American Historical Review* 105 (April 2000): 417–50.
    NOTE   This is a citation to an entire article. If only a portion of the article is being cited, just give that page or page range.

Magazine article

7   Bruce Bower, "Trailing Lewis and Clark," Science News, September 26, 1998, 205.

Newspaper article

8   Patt Morrison, "France and California: Vive the differences and similarities," *Los Angeles Times*, June 20, 2001, Section B, p. 3.
    NOTE   If no author is given, just provide the other information.

Encyclopedia article

9   *Signed article*
    Peter N. Stearns, "Social history," in *A Global Encyclopedia of Historical Writing*.
10 *Unsigned article*
    The New Century Classical Handbook, s.v. "Golden apples of the Hesperides."

Essay (chapter)

11 Anthony Brundage, "Private charity and the 1834 Poor Law," in Donald T. Critchlow and Charles H. Parker (eds.), *With Us always: Private Charity and Public Assistance in Historical Perspective* (Lanham, MD: Rowman & Littlefield, 1998), 108.

Book review

12 Lesley Abrams, review of *Kingship and Government in Pre-Conquest England, c. 500–1066*, by Ann Williams, *Albion* 32 (2000): 467.

Other Types of Sources

Dissertation

13 Michael Steven Smith, "*Anti-radical expression: Counter-revolutionary thought in the age of revolution*" (PhD dissertation, University of California, Riverside, 1999), 132.

Government document

14   United States Commission on Civil Rights, *Civil Rights '63: 1963 Report of the United States Commission on Civil Rights* (Washington: GPO, 1963), 209.

Website

15   Lynn McDonald, "Collected works of Florence Nightingale: Introduction to the project," 1998. Available from http://www.anthropology.uoguelph.ca/fnightingale/introduction.htm (accessed 21 June 2001).

Videorecording

16   *The Architecture of Frank Lloyd Wright*, Barbara and Murray Grigor (producers), Murray Grigor (writer and director), 75 min. Direct Cinema Limited, 1993. Videocassette.

Footnote Reference to a Previously Cited Work

When making a subsequent citation to a work previously cited in an earlier footnote/endnote, do not repeat all the information. Use a short form, the simplest of which is the author's surname followed by the page reference. If, however, there is more than one work by that author in your bibliography, you need to add a short version of the title. If you had already cited, say, Stephen E. Ambrose's book *Undaunted Courage: Meriwether Lewis, Thomas Jefferson, and the Opening of the American West*, then you would not have to repeat all this, or the publication data, in a subsequent note. Assuming that there were no other works by this author in your bibliography, you could cite it the following way:

17   Ambrose, 193.

While this is the most streamlined of the acceptable forms, it is best to use a short title, something you would have to do if you had more than one book by Stephen Ambrose in your bibliography:

18   Ambrose, *Undaunted Courage*, 193.

If there was another author in your bibliography with the same surname, you would need to provide the first name in order to avoid confusion. It is also acceptable to use "ibid." (an abbreviation of the Latin word *ibidem*, meaning "in the same place"), but only when the footnote/endnote that contains it comes immediately after the full citation of the work to which "ibid." refers. For example, supposing that "19" and "20" in our list are two note numbers:

19   Stephen E. Ambrose, *Undaunted Courage: Meriwether Lewis, Thomas Jefferson, and the Opening of the American West* (New York: Simon & Schuster, 1996), 88.

20   Ibid., 193.

Appendix D
Bibliography Formatting

The key to understanding bibliography formatting is that materials are organized alphabetically, usually by authors' surnames.

Book

McLaughlin, Andrew Cunningham. *America and Britain*. New York: E. P. Dutton, 1919.

Article

Benjamin, Thomas. "A time of reconquest: History, the Maya revival, and the Zapatista rebellion in Chiapas." *American Historical Review* 105 (2000): 417–50.

Essay (chapter)

Brundage, Anthony. "Private charity and the 1834 Poor Law." In Donald T. Critchlow and Charles H. Parker (eds.), *With Us always: Private Charity and Public Assistance in Historical Perspective*, 99–119. Lanham, MD: Rowman & Littlefield, 1998.

Dissertation

Smith, Michael Steven. "Anti-radical expression: Counter-revolutionary thought in the age of revolution." PhD dissertation, University of California, Riverside, 1999.

Sample bibliography

Bibliography entries should have hanging indentation. In the Chicago style, a period, not a comma, should follow the author's name, as well as the title of the work. Unlike in footnotes/endnotes, in a bibliography parentheses are not used to enclose place of publication, publisher, and date. The following sample contains titles of secondary sources. In a research paper, primary sources are generally listed separately and appear before the secondary sources. Primary sources in the form of books, articles, and chapters follow the same rules as secondary materials do.

Anstruther, Ian. *The Scandal of the Andover Workhouse*. 2nd ed. Gloucester: Sutton, 1984.

Apfel, William, and Peter Dunkley. "English rural society and the new Poor Law: Bedfordshire, 1834–1847." *Social History* 10 (1985): 37–68.

Bartlett, Peter. "The asylum, the workhouse, and the voice of the insane poor in 19th-century England." *International Journal of Law and Psychiatry* 21 (1998): 421–32.

Brundage, Anthony. *The English Poor Laws, 1700–1930*. New York: Palgrave, 2001.

Choomwattana, Chakrit. *"The opposition to the new Poor Law in Sussex, 1834–1837."* PhD dissertation, Cornell University, Ithaca, New York, 1986.

Cody, Lisa Forman. "The politics of illegitimacy in an age of reform: Women, reproduction, and political economy in England's new Poor Law of 1834." *Journal of Women's History* 11 (2000): 131–56.

Daunton, M. J. *Progress and Poverty: An Economic and Social History of Britain, 1700–1850*. Oxford: Oxford University Press, 1995.

Fido, Judith. "The Charity Organisation Society and social casework in London 1869–1900." In A. P. Donajgrodzki, ed., *Social Control in Nineteenth-Century Britain*, 207–30. London: Croom Helm, 1977.

Appendix D 151

Franzén, Katharine Mary Grigsby. *"Free to leave: Government assisted emigration under the 1834 Poor Law."* PhD dissertation, University of Virginia, Charlottesville, Virginia, 1996.

Huzel, James P. "The labourer and the Poor Law, 1750–1850." In G. E. Mingay, ed., *The Agrarian History of England and Wales*, vol. 6: *1750–1850*, 755–810. Cambridge: Cambridge University Press, 1989.

Jones, Margaret. "The 1908 Old Age Pensions Act: The Poor Law in new disguise?" In Keith Laybourn, ed., *Social Conditions, Status, and Community, 1860–c.1920*, 82–103. Stroud: Sutton, 1997.

Landau, Norma. "The eighteenth-century context of the laws of settlement." Continuity and Change 6 (1991): 417–39.

Lees, Lynn Hollen. *The Solidarities of Strangers: The English Poor Laws and the People, 1700–1948*. Cambridge: Cambridge University Press, 1998.

Levine-Clark, Marjorie. "Engendering relief: Women, ablebodiedness, and the new Poor Law in early Victorian England." *Journal of Women's History* 11 (2000): 107–30.

Melling, Joseph, Richard Adair, and Bill Forsythe. "'A proper lunatic for two years': Pauper lunatic children in Victorian and Edwardian England: Child admissions to the Devon County Asylum, 1845–1914." *Journal of Social History* 31 (1997): 371–405.

Poynter, J. R. *Society and Pauperism: English Ideas on Poor Relief, 1795–1834*. London: Routledge & Kegan Paul, 1969.

Richardson, Ruth. *Death, Dissection, and the Destitute*. London: Routledge & Kegan Paul, 1987.

Rose, Mary Beth. "Social policy and business: Parish apprenticeship and the factory system, 1750– 1834." *Business History* 31 (1989): 5–32.

Song, Byung Khun. "Agrarian policies on pauper settlement and migration, Oxfordshire, 1750–1834." *Continuity and Change* 13 (1998): 363–89.

Vorspan, Rachel. "Vagrancy and the new Poor Law in late Victorian and Edwardian England." *English Historical Review* 92 (1977): 59–81.

Webb, Sidney, and Beatrice Webb. *English Poor Law History. Part II: The Last Hundred Years*. 2 vols. London: Longmans Green, 1929.

Winch, Donald. *Riches and Poverty: An Intellectual History of Political Economy in Britain, 1750–1834*. Cambridge: Cambridge University Press, 1996.

Appendix E
Commonly Used Abbreviations

anon.	anonymous
app.	appendix
art.	article
b.	born
c.	copyright, copy, or *circa* (see next entry)
ca.	*circa*, around, approximately, as in ca. 1834
cf.	*confer*, compare, a suggestion that the reader compare two or more works
ch. (or chap.)	chapter (plural chs.)
col.	column (plural, cols.)
d.	died
diss.	dissertation
e.g.	*exempli gratia*, for example
et al.	*et alia*, and other things/*et alii*, and others
et seq.	*et sequens*, and the following one/*et sequentia*, *et sequentes*, and the following ones
fig.	figure
fl.	*floruit*, used when birth and death dates are unknown

Going to the Sources: A Guide to Historical Research and Writing, Fifth Edition.
Anthony Brundage.
© 2013 John Wiley & Sons, Ltd. Published 2013 by John Wiley & Sons, Ltd.

ibid.	*ibidem*, in the same place
id.	*idem*, the same person, usually referring to an author
i.e.	*id est*, that is
ill.	illustrated or illustration
infra	below, a reference to a later point in the work
l. or ll.	line or lines
n.	footnote or endnote (plural nn.)
n.d.	no date of publication provided
no.	number
n.p.	no place of publication or no publisher provided
n.s.	new series
op. cit.	*opere citato*, in the work cited
o.s.	old series
p.	page (plural pp.)
par.	paragraph (plural, pars.)
passim	here and there throughout the work
pseud.	pseudonym
pt.	part (plural, pts.)
q.v.	*quod vide*, which see, indicating a cross-reference
rev.	revised
sec.	section
sic	so (in the original) – placed in brackets after an error or misspelling in a quotation, to indicate that the text indeed appears in that form in the original
supp. or suppl.	supplement
supra	above – a reference to an earlier point in the work
s.v.	*sub verbo*, under the word, referring to an encyclopedia entry
trans.	translator or translated by
viz.	*videlicet*, namely
vol. or v.	volume

Suggestions for Further Reading

The following short list of books represents only a small portion of the many valuable texts and reference works that might be of service to students of history. Each book is apt to prove valuable for different aspects of research and writing.

Appleby, Joyce, Lynn Hunt, and Margaret Jacob. *Telling the Truth about History*. New York and London: W. W. Norton & Co., 1995. An incisive analysis of the impact of scientific thinking and the concept of objectivity on historians in the modern era; this work includes a thoughtful discussion of postmodernism's challenge to modern historiography.

Barzun, Jacques, and Henry Graff. *The Modern Researcher*. 6th ed. Belmont, CA: Thomson/Wadsworth, 2004. A classic in the field, this lengthy, well-written guide by two masters of the historian's craft is particularly useful for its exploration of the intellectual processes involved in researching and writing history.

Breisach, Ernst. *Historiography, Ancient, Medieval, and Modern*. 3rd ed. Chicago, IL: University of Chicago Press, 2007. An excellent survey text of the history of historical writing from the ancient world to the twentieth century.

Going to the Sources: A Guide to Historical Research and Writing, Fifth Edition.
Anthony Brundage.
© 2013 John Wiley & Sons, Ltd. Published 2013 by John Wiley & Sons, Ltd.

Conkin, Paul K., and Roland H. Stromberg. *Heritage and Challenge: The History and Theory of History*. Wheeling, IL: Harlan Davidson, Inc., 1989. Combines a brief yet scholarly history of historical writing with a concise, sophisticated analysis of the major philosophical and theoretical issues confronting historians today.

Furay, Conal, and Michael J. Salevouris. *The Methods and Skills of History: A Practical Guide*. 3rd ed. Wheeling, IL: Harlan Davidson, Inc., 2010. A good methods text/workbook that combines theory with "hands-on" practice.

Gilderhus, Mark T. *History and Historians: A Historiographical Introduction*. 5th ed. Upper Saddle River, NJ: Prentice-Hall, 2003. A concise, lucid introduction to the history of historical writing as well as to some of the basics of research.

Hexter, J. H. *Doing History*. Bloomington, IN: Indiana University Press, 1971. A lively, offbeat explication of history as a form of knowledge, exploring its inner dynamics as well as its relationship to other disciplines. Stresses the distinctiveness of history and its fundamental differences from the social sciences.

McMichael, Andrew. *History on the Web: Using and Evaluating the Internet*. Wheeling, IL: Harlan Davidson, Inc., 2005. A brief, highly effective guide to finding and assessing internet sites in history.

Mann, Thomas. *The Oxford Guide to Library Research*. New York: Oxford University Press, 2005. A detailed exploration of various research strategies and resources.

Strunk, William Jr., and E. B. White. *The Elements of Style*. 4th ed. Boston, MA: Allyn & Bacon, 2000. A classic in its own right that explores the subject of style, urging and helping the reader to write with wit, verve, and style. A particularly good guide to commonly misused words and phrases.

Turabian, Kate L. *A Manual for Writers of Term Papers, Theses, and Dissertations*. 7th ed. Chicago, IL: University of Chicago Press, 2007. Based on the *University of Chicago Manual of Style*, this short reference work covers all aspects of citing and formatting, not just for history and the social sciences but for the natural sciences as well.

Index

Going to the Sources: A Guide to Historical Research and Writing, Fifth Edition.
Anthony Brundage.
© 2013 John Wiley & Sons, Ltd. Published 2013 by John Wiley & Sons, Ltd.